We Will Remember

World War Two Veterans

Wild Tweed Limited

ISBN 978-0-9957816-2-7

Photography - All Colour Photography © Matt Limb

Published By
Wild Tweed Limited

We Will Remember

World War Two Veterans

Matt Limb

Foreword

This book has taken me over thirty years to get to print; or to be more exact, the idea for this book started about thirty years ago. At that time, I watched the surviving soldiers from World War One slipping away, taking with them their stories. People argued with me that we had their service records, but service records were not their stories, their thoughts, their experiences, or their fears.

Slowly they all slipped away, as they shifted from living memory into history. But the idea of capturing the stories of World War Two soldiers came into my mind, hoping to not allow history to repeat itself, which sadly, it has a habit of doing.

So, after several false starts, I began looking for and capturing the stories of World War Two Veterans. It was never practical or possible to capture them all, but I believe the veterans I had the privileged to meet and whose stories I have preserved, show the character of a generation born a century ago.

They are a generation that has seen profound change, many speak of fathers and uncles serving in The Great War. Yet hardly a generation later they were to answer the call of the country in another war.

The veterans in this book served in the Royal Navy, Army and Royal Air Force along with the ATS. They all joined up after the outbreak of war, they wanted to do something for their country, at a time referred to by Winston Churchill as our darkest hour.

Between them, they witnessed the North Africa campaign, Italy, D Day and the Rhine Crossing leading to VE Day, even the concentration camps. Others were in the far east still confronting the Japanese even after VJ Day as they visited the numerous remote islands.

But this is not a collection of war stories. They are stories of amazing people leading amazing lives. Yet, none of them regard themselves as heroes or believe they did anything special, they just did what was expected of them, for their country.

Matt Limb OBE TD   November 2022

This book is dedicated to all veterans
Never counting the cost, never questioning the cause
We Will Remember

Contents

Jack Smith
Royal Marines

I met up with Jack in a small care home where he is one of just twelve residents, Jack had only been living here for the past fifteen months, before that living by himself at home. Sat chatting with Jack he was still a proud man, admitting he was especially pleased of his time during World War Two and his actions on D Day in 1944, where he played a vital role as the coxswain on a landing craft.

Jack was born on Valentine's Day, 14 February 1925, in Hinckley, Leicestershire, his parents were Harry and Clara who was known as 'click' which is believed to come from her work as a clicker in a hosiery mill, while Harry worked in a shoe factory. Jack's father had served in the Great War of 1914 – 1918 and while Jack did not know his regiment, he was always told he worked with the horses and has a picture in his room of him from World War One.

Jack was their youngest child, he grew up with his brother, Sidney, who was nine years older; there was another brother, Eric, who sadly died as an infant and Jack never knew him. Sid, as he was always known, worked at the Co-op grocery shop only leaving when he was conscripted during World War Two and served with the Royal Artillery.

Jack started school at five, then at eleven went to Westfield Secondary School before leaving at fourteen, he admits to enjoying school and playing football for the school.

On leaving school, like so many in the town, he started working at a local

factory that made stockings and socks, he stayed in the same job until he joined up.

Aged just seventeen Jack volunteered and joined the Royal Marines in 1942. He intended to join the Royal Navy, but the Navy Recruiting Officer told him he was too young, sending him up the road to the Royal Marines.

Some years ago, Jack wrote of his experiences, from joining up, to his time with the Royal Marines and I feel privileged that he and his daughter Carol, were happy to share his notes with me as we chatted.

Jack's notes started on the day he received his call up papers, which his mum gave to him as he was sitting eating his dinner.

'It was an exciting time; I went out to tell all my mates.

'Then 3rd April arrived, I went to Leicester to meet the recruiting officer at the railway station and he saw me off with two other Leicester lads, 17-year-old Tom Fletcher and Joe Turner. We went via London to South Barracks in Deal; we were only there for a week to get kitted up and to be read the riot act.'

'After a week in Deal, we were put on a train for London and then north-west to Whitley Bay in Northumberland. About halfway to London, our train was attacked by German aircraft, which dropped bombs and machine-gunned the train. We were in marching order so diving for cover was a bit difficult, the sound of the bullets hitting all around was very frightening and the attack lasted as far as I can remember for about five minutes. There were a few casualties, but the train was still in one piece, so it continued to London where ambulances were waiting.

Jack made his way safely to Whitley Bay but was surprised when he arrived to be billeted in a private house which had been requisitioned by the government for troop accommodation.

'We were there for six weeks learning the basics of small arms and explosives and of course drill. At the end of the six weeks, I got myself a Red Diamond which meant I was going to an NCO Course.

'I was sent to what is now Butlins holiday camp at Scarborough, it was not finished then, it was just plain huts. Then followed another six-weeks of

small arms, grenades and taking charge of drill squads. After passing out I was promoted to Lance Corporal.

'At this stage, I must point out that at 17-years-old we were not going to the front-line jobs but the defence of the Royal Naval Air Stations. After Butlins, I went to a stone frigate [a shore base] HMS Gosling near Leigh in Lancashire, on arrival I was promoted to full Corporal and sent home on my first leave.

'I could hardly wait to get home, very excited, I arrived at Hinckley station at about 7 am where my dad met me and we were walking home. I was telling him all about it then suddenly (bearing in mind I was wearing full marching order) I knew something was missing.

'My rifle, I left the bloody rifle on the train. Talk about panic stations.

Jack after being promoted to Corporal

'I went straight back to the railway station to report what I had done then to the police station. Needless to say, Saturday was a nightmare going back without my rifle, a Canadian P14 very accurate for shooting, long barrel, but useless for drill with the short butt.

'Anyway, somebody suggested I go to the Salvation Army in Hinckley which I did, well I must admit I had little faith in getting it back, but I was everlasting grateful when I was woken on Sunday morning by my dad to be told that the 'Sally' had got my rifle back.

'What a relief; that's why today over fifty years on I will always put a donation into the Sally Army box'

'Back to HMS Gosling, after about 4 weeks we were posted to Crail Naval Station in Fife Scotland as station defence, we were all seventeen-year-olds not quite what we had in mind but better than anything at home, so we thought, we did the usual routine of drill, shooting, PT and lectures.

'At the weekends you could put your name down for a flight in a Swordfish aircraft in the gunner's seat whilst they were being tested, as they were aircraft from carriers that were in for repair. I did this once it was quite an experience open cockpit, flying helmet and hanging on for life talk about a white-knuckle ride.

After a few more months in Scotland, Jack was on the move again, back to Deal in Kent, this time for a seamanship course, but just before he departed, he was *'selected'* for another task, the station boxing team.

'I was selected for the station boxing team to fight another station from Arbroath, I fought an Irish salior, Paddy [I can't remember his second name] I didn't really want to do it, but as I said I was selected. I got a right going over, everybody said I did very well, but looking in the mirror I did not think so.

'After the seamanship course, we were sent to HMS Effingham to join Combined Operations, this was the name suggested to a force formed to use all the three services on Special Operations together.

'I was sent for training on landing craft, then to a flotilla of LCV(P) Landing Craft Vehicle Personnel, which meant I could carry either men or vehicles.

'I was a coxswain, along with a stoker driver who looked after the engine and a deckhand.

Chatting with Jack he could not remember the name of his crew but could clearly remember the deckhand as being older than him and coming from Yorkshire.

'I was posted to HMS Sea Serpent at Bracklesham Bay, another stone frigate, then after a few months we sailed our craft along the south coast into Poole harbour and after tying up we were ferried to HMS Turtle.

Jack spoke about an afternoon when he and his landing craft were on duty, noting that 1272 was the number of his Landing Craft.

> '1272 had been duty craft out in the Solent and we decided to go ashore at Cowes for a quick cup of tea in the local WVS Canteen. I tied her up to the pier and off we went. I forgot to check the tide table so about an hour later when we arrived back there was 1272 hanging on the pier of Cowes and the Pier Master doing his nut. Anyway, we had to wait for the tide to come in which took about two or three hours before we could get off. I got put on report but that was the last I heard of it.

Whilst at HMS Turtle, located in Poole Harbour, a World War Two Landing Craft Training Establishment, Jack's life would take another unexpected turn; it was March 1944.

> 'After settling at Turtle, I along with a few mates went ashore into the town of Poole. Footloose and fancy-free, where were all the girls? At the dance, at the Centenary Hall above the Labour Club. I forgot how many times I'd been to the dance but after about two weeks I was there one night when this girl walked in, she looks quite nice, so I asked her for a dance.

> 'She said no thank you, anyway just then I noticed another girl who must have come in with her, because they were both wearing identical jumpers, hand knitted. She was lovely so I asked her for a dance, she said yes, well I tell you I fell head over heels for this girl. I asked if I could walk her home, but she said no because she was with another marine.

> 'I went back to the Centenary Hall dance a few nights later and low and behold who should be there but this lovely girl, this time she was alone. After having most of the dances with her I once again asked her if I could take her home and this time she said yes. Her name was Betty Sylvia Dennis, she told me she lived in Rockley Road, Hamworthy, Poole.

> 'Off we went and walked about one and a half miles in the blackout, lovely. We finally arrived at the bottom of Tuckers Lane which leads to Rockley Road and after a little small talk I kissed her and oh boy I knew she was the one for me.

> 'We arrange to meet the next night by the school at the top of the lane, I could hardly wait to get ashore that night. But after reaching the school I waited on the opposite side of the road. I saw her walk up the lane and

who should be walking down the road but 'Tiny Thompson' the other marine, he saw her walking up and waited for her.

'There was I on the other side of the road fuming, so I turned and walked into town - eating the chocolate ration I had saved for her.

'The next day draft orders were posted we were sailing the flotilla to Exbury on the Beaulieu River to HMS Mastodon. I did not want to lose Betty, so I wrote a letter explaining what was happening and went to the dance hall that night. I'd already been to the factory I thought she worked, only to be told she had left. When I got to the dance there she was, she explained that Tiny - we later were the best of pals - turning up the night before was an accident and that she had made an excuse and went back home.

'So, I gave her the letter and explain what was happening, not where we were going because at that stage I didn't know myself. We parted that night in Tuckers Lane promising to write to each other.

The Exbury Estate, in the New Forest, performed a critical role before D Day, the estate and house were designated as HMS Mastodon from May 1942 until the end of the war. Amongst other responsibilities, HMS Mastodon was responsible for the administration, arming and training of crews on landing craft for D Day.

'Next day we climbed aboard our landing craft in line headed and sailed out of the needles to starboard and set course for the Beaulieu River which we went along till we reached Exbury and tied up and went ashore to the camp which was HMS Mastodon. We were living under canvas in tents in the grounds of Exbury house.

'The whole setup was top security, special operations training. It was now the beginning of May 1944. The weather was pretty good, and would you believe it the Petty Officer WREN in the galley was a Hinckley girl who I knew from the working man's club days, her name was Dorothy Hopewell.

'We knew by our training along the south coast and the build-up of forces in the area something big was being planned. The Solent was filling up with troopships, so many in fact that you can almost walk from the mainland to the IOW and the New Forest had a huge build-up of tanks and men.

Jack now promoted to Sergeant following D Day

'Then one day I was detailed for a guard of honour; we did not know who was coming and I was rather hoping it would be Winston Churchill. But when the day arrives who would step out of the car in front of me at Exbury House but HM King George VI. I must admit I felt rather proud as the king walked past.

'I remember 4th June 1944; everybody was mustard after being given the news we will be going to invade France along the coast of Normandy. Reserve crews were dispatched to Southampton to relieve us later, we collected all our gear and went aboard our craft. I was still only nineteen so this was a big buzz. Down the river we sailed, but after about two hours we heaved too and return to Beaulieu and Exbury. The reason was an eight gale in the channel, the whole invasion had been postponed, you can imagine the problems that caused for security.

'Next day at about 2300hrs off we went again, still very rough. We were being tossed all over the place I had my sea legs, so I felt fine, but I felt sorry for the soldiers on the troopers some of them were very ill. After joining the circus at the NAB Tower off we set in line and headed for Normandy.

'After a very rough crossing, we arrived to find all hell breaking loose. The next few days changed me from a young boy into a man. When you see death and destruction all around it gives you a whole new outlook on life.

'Anyway, we carried men and materials ashore expecting every time we ran in to hit a mine, quite a lot of landing craft were lost that way. There was a lot of bodies floating in the sea, I do not mind admitting I was scared, thank goodness we had air superiority. There was the odd German plane coming over dropping bombs and strafing with their machine guns.

'To give a temporary harbour cover, old tramp steamers were bought over and sunk off Arromanches, these were called the Gooseberries. A week later they bought the Mulberries, these were large concrete caissons which they joined together to form a better harbour and ran a floating jetty from the beach.

'By this time men and supplies were pouring in, one day I was outside the Mulberry Harbour when we saw what looked like a huge bobbin being towed, it was unwinding a flexible pipe as it came, it was PLUTO. The Pipe Line Under The Ocean - used to pump fuel across from the UK.

Talking with Jack he remembers running his landing craft onto all the beaches, both British and American. He was given orders to take troops ashore, Jack and his crew moved little if any cargo or general equipment, even today he still has no idea who the troops were.

Jack remembered a second storm, which is certainly the storm in the Channel that started on 19th June 1944. The storm severely damaged the Mulberry Harbour being assembled off Omaha Beach, known as Mulberry A or Mulberry American. It was judged to be irreparable and abandoned, as all future efforts put into the Mulberry Harbour at Arromanches.

'About two weeks after D-Day I had been up the American beach at Omaha [Beach] about twenty miles up the coast, on the way back we hit a storm, they later said after it was a force eight. The gearbox on my craft,

*which was LCV(P) 1272, a number I
will never forget, packed in so we were
left hanging on for dear life for about
24-hours. Lucky for us the storm blew
us towards the Mulberry Harbour and
after it died down, we were spotted and
towed in.*

Jack, along with his crew, stayed with
LCV(P) 1272 in France until September,
continually working along the invasion
beaches, before crossing The Channel
and returning to England in a floating
dock, or a dock ship, it was the first time
Jack had seen a floating dock.

*'Into the dock ship and our journey back
to the UK, I could hardly believe it as
we steamed into Poole harbour and
unloaded our landing craft and lined
up on the Sandbanks Yacht Club.*

Jack & Betty's Wedding Day
April 1945

*'There I left 1272. She was my home for the past four months, how I wish
I had taken a small piece of her as a souvenir, we had been through a lot
together.*

*'After climbing onto the lorries, we were taken to HMS Turtle at Poole, we
had a meal at the base then I asked permission to go ashore and see Betty.
I went to Rockley Road and there she was, it was grand to see her again.*

*'Later I met the rest of the lads at Poole railway station and after saying
bye to Betty, off they took us to Southampton.*

*'Later came some home leave, Betty came up to Hinckley from her home in
Poole to my mum and dad's; straight away they liked her.*

*'After this, I went to various bases all over the country, then I was sent to
Southend-on-Sea and later got married. I only had a long weekend, so the
wedding had to be on Friday, 13th April 1945. It was a lovely day with
the reception in the front room of 107 Factory Road, and the vicar who
married us came along.*

Jack and Betty married close to Jack's parent's home in Hinckley at Saint Mary's Church, they married shortly before VE Day and the end of the war in Europe.

> 'I went back to Southend-on-Sea on the Sunday and a few days later got made up to Sergeant. As a Senior NCO I could sleep out, so I sent for Betty she came down and stayed with me for a few weeks. Then got drafted to Inveraray in Scotland again on landing craft; this was about August 1945.

> 'In January 1946, Betty's father Steve passed away, I had met him a few times but never really got to know him, I remember we went to the funeral.

Betty's mother, who was known as Jane had died from TB some years before, Betty's lasting memory of her was leaving in an ambulance when she was aged nine.

> 'I went back to Scotland until March 1946, then I got drafted to an aircraft carrier, HMS Chaser, at Fraserburgh in Scotland. But before I could get there, I was drafted back to Pompeii for my demob.

> 'I came out in May 1946, we went to Blackpool for a week with my brother Sid, his wife Ethel and their daughter Jill. The war was over and we now wanted to get on with the rest of our lives.

I asked Jack if he thought about staying in the Royal Marines after the war for a full career; but he said he simply wanted to get home to Betty, who was still living with his Mum and Dad in Hinckley.

> 'Looking back now on those days, whilst I have had a good experience of being in the war, I feel now I missed out on my teenage years in the special sense, it was all blackouts and rationing.

> 'But at least I came back which is more than a lot of my school and fellow townspeople did.

> 'I often go to the Argents Mead [War] Memorial [in Hinckley] and look at the names I can put faces to and say hello to the ones that I knew.

Jack settled back into his civilian life, returning to his old job at Moore and Osbornes in Druid Street, Hinckley, again working in a hosiery factory.

In February 1947 Jack and Betty moved from 107 Factory Road with his parents and bought a house in Westfield Road, still in Hinckley, next door to his brother.

Jack clearly remembers the awful winter of 1947 when everything came to a standstill with power cuts and roads blocked, he commented that life was still hard with many items on ration. But they settled into their new home and then on 13th May their first baby arrived, Janice.

In 1949 Jack and Betty's only son was born, who was named Eric, after the brother that Jack never knew, following Eric they had two more daughters Carol and Suzanne. Looking at his wider family today, Jack has eleven grandchildren and thirteen great-grandchildren.

Jack always had a love of music and played in a band when his children were young, in the early 1960s Jack formed a band 'The Eric Jackson Five' the name coming from Eric being Jack's son who joined his dad on the keyboard.

Most of Jack and Betty's children were involved in the band which entertained people most weekends and became a family event, as they played in local working men's clubs, at weddings and private parties.

Jack finally retired in 1990 aged 65, after finishing work in a knitwear factory, soon he and Betty enjoyed retirement together.

Sadly, Betty was diagnosed with dementia and her health started to fail, she passed away peacefully on New Year's Eve 2017, Jack and Betty had been married for over 72 years.

Jack continued to live by himself for another three years until he moved into his current care home, just over a year ago.

A few weeks after meeting Jack, which was so enjoyable, I received a message from his daughter Carol to say Jack had sadly passed away, but his story should still be told, as that was his wish.

Tom Carter
Royal Artillery

I met up with Tom, born Charles Thomas Carter but always known as Tom, in his hometown of Loughborough, where he was born and has been a resident most of his life, now living comfortably in an independent retirement apartment.

It was soon very apparent that given his age of ninety-eight years, Tom has led not only a full life but has taken every opportunity it has thrown at him and dare I say, enjoyed most of it, even today he has a very positive outlook.

> 'My dad's name was Thomas Carter, he was a farm labourer near Oxford there was only farm labouring around Oxford those days, so he started building work for the Central Railway, he went to work on that for more money. He worked on the central railway until he got to Loughborough, doing the embankments and that.
>
> 'My mum's name was Violetta Priestley, between them they had seven daughters, I was the only son and the youngest, but two other children were lost in infancy.
>
> 'My father did not serve in World War One, but I had an uncle, Uncle Chris my mother's brother, he was called up to the Leicestershire Regiment and became a casualty with no known grave but is remembered at the Tyne Cott Cemetery [memorial], his name is on panel fifty or fifty-one.

'What happened was the colonel gathered all the men together and repulsed an attack, but they were all killed including the colonel, it was October 1917.

Research soon found Tom's uncle; Private Christopher Priestley, who on joining up gave his home address as Loughborough, Leicestershire, he died on 1st October 1917, serving with the 9th Battalion the Leicestershire Regiment, a Pal's Battalion raised early in the war and disbanded in 1918.

As Tom remembers, he has no known grave but is commemorated on the Tyne Cot Memorial, in Belgium. Interesting are Tom's comments about his Colonel being killed whilst repulsing an enemy attack.

This is almost certainly Lieutenant Colonel Philip Eric Bent VC, DSO, Commanding Officer of the 9th Battalion, aged twenty-six when he was killed on 1st October 1917, whilst leading a counterattack.

It was an action for which he was awarded the Victoria Cross. Part of his Victoria Cross Citation reads; '... *This very gallant officer was killed whilst leading a charge which he inspired with the call of Come on the Tigers.* The Leicestershire Regiment's nickname is - The Tigers.

Returning to Tom, he continued his story.

'I was born in Loughborough near the entrance to the park, my father's first wife Sarah Ann died in 1901, and then he met my mother. I went to Emmanuel School in Victoria Street at five, then I went to Warner Street School, I failed my eleven plus exam so went to Limehurst Boys School, all in Loughborough. Warner school has been knocked down, but the headmistress's house is still there. I did not enjoy school 'cos I couldn't spell, and they never bothered with me, but I enjoyed school for drawing but hated school 'cos I could not spell, I had seven sisters, and no one helped me.

'I still draw today; it helps occupy my time and is good therapy.

'I can only remember one family holiday, near Banbury we went to a place called North Newington, which is where my dad went to school, we were split up between the family but me being the youngest I slept with my mum and dad, staying with the posh one of the family, I was about thirteen.

Tom with his Sisters and Parents

'Then where my dad worked at the builders, Barkers in Loughborough, every year they had a family trip to the seaside, just for the one day and we always got a shilling [five pence], we went to Skegness or Cleethorpes, we caught the train from Loughborough.

'As teenagers they [my sisters] worked in hosiery factories, it was only when the war came, they moved into engineering, a lot of them went to Morris the crane maker, but none of them served in uniform in World War Two.

'I left school at fourteen my mother did not want me to be like my father he was a labourer and yard man at a local builder, but he was a good one, my dad wanted me to work in the brickyard and get my hands rough as a bricklayer, but my mother did not want that.

'So, I went to work in this shop, there was a man who had three or four shops in Loughborough, so I went to work as a shop assistant, in Church Gate, Loughborough.

'At the back of the shop was a pawn shop, and people would come in on a Monday morning bringing in their best suits, getting enough money for the week, then on a Friday night they would come in and redeem them.

'I worked from eight in the morning till seven thirty at night with two breaks, Wednesday was a half day, then Saturday we worked till nine.

'There were three shops, the first shop was a working man's shop, overalls and wellingtons and that. The middle shop did better men's clothing, the third shop was a jewellery shop, they moved me around all the shops, then as the older men got called up [to the war] I got moved up.

During my time with Tom, I found he was creative not only at drawing, which he still enjoys, but also, in his day, a talented singer.

'I would be about eight when my mother volunteered me to be a choirboy, at Emmanuel Church, we got a shilling [five pence] for a funeral and a wedding, then the church paid you about three and six [seventeen and a half pence] every quarter, I stayed till my voice broke aged about fifteen.

'On the morning of Sunday 3rd September 1939, I was in church as normal, being top lad in the choir.

'The sidesman came in during the service and spoke to the vicar who announced that the country was now at war with Germany.

'After the service, I went to the drill hall on Granby Street to see if there were many soldiers there, but there were only about half a dozen drilling. At five o'clock the siren went. After 10 minutes the all-clear sounded – a false alarm.

'The first 6 months were what they called the phoney war and apart from streetlamps being blacked out and blackout curtains put up, nothing affected my life.

'During that winter as air raids or the threat of them increased, people had to take turns fire watching. We had to congregate at the Victory Cinema at the end of Dead Lane where the bus station was built. We slept on bunks and when the siren went off had to patrol the streets in pairs. This was organised through my work, but similar patrols worked in residential areas. You were on duty every eighth night and of course, had to be up ready for work the next morning despite a disturbed night.

'In 1941 I became old enough to join the Civil Defence. I wanted to join a first aid party but first I had to pass a course, so also joined the

St John's Ambulance Brigade. The ambulance service in Loughborough was done by St John's. The crew for manning Loughborough Ambulance Service was only two men, so young members of the Brigade spent as much time as we could spare as ambulance attendants, as well as every sixth night on duty.

'I experienced a range of incidents, from expectant mothers who had been evacuated to Loughborough from the cities. Joyce in the flat upstairs was one of these, to accidents as well as routine trips to the hospital.

One significant experience was witnessing a post-mortem. Pat Collins, an ambulance driver

Tom on Fire Watch

and superintendent of the Brigade, asked us in turn if we wanted to witness a post-mortem – as everyone else did, so I did.

'Another time my mate was on duty when a call came in that a girl had been knocked off a bike.

'We found her lying in the road and Cal Prince had a look at her. She was bleeding from the ears nose and mouth, but I knew we had to get her to the hospital as quickly as possible. When I went down the next day, she had fractured ribs and collar bone, as well as concussion.

'I can remember walking home on Beacon Road watching the light in the sky from Coventry [being bombing] it lasted for over twelve hours.

'But I knew, in the blackout that if I counted thirty-five steps from the corner I was at my house. I can also remember standing in Baxter Gate and watching the fires in Leicester and standing with my dad before I joined the civil defence, looking over Nottingham and it was red.

I asked Tom if he could remember Loughborough being bombed:

'Off Beacon Road was a field, one night this plane flew over low and dropped four bombs there were houses each side and they landed in the middle of the field and didn't do any damage.

'Then on the Coventry raid, about eleven at night, this plane came over and crashed at Six Hills, all the crew got killed. It was part of our team that went out that night and picked the bodies up.

In August 1942 Tom was called-up, he was eighteen years old. He signed on at the Post Office, wishing to join the Royal Army Medical Corps, but the army had different ideas. Soon Tom received instructions to join the 32nd Primary Training Unit at Alexandria in Scotland and was issued with a train warrant.

'My call up came 18th August 1942, then I had to go for a medical in Leicester and was graded A2, 'cos I had a varicose vein in my leg. Then on 5th November 1942 I left home, I went to see my mates and had a good haircut, then two of my sisters, Amy and Violet, walked me down to the station to see me off, I didn't want them to come.

'I went on the two o'clock train, which was two in the morning. I got on and was walking through the corridor and didn't shut a door when someone shouted 'shut that bloody door' it was full of soldiers. That train ran every night through the war, it was very handy to get home.

'The barracks was an old factory, with twenty platoons, all split into sections. The lad in the next bed to me deserted I woke up one morning and he was gone, I did not see him again, except at a distance when he was bought back.

'I had six weeks basic training which involved doing foot drill, hours on end, firing a .303 rifle, a Bren gun and I used one hand grenade - though in fact I never had to use one after - plus scrubbing the gym floor. There were also injections and I remember skating to breakfast on the slippery road because the cobblestones were so icy.

'Another experience was the gas chamber, poisonous gas was released; we had to remove our masks and walk around coughing and spitting. Then mustard gas was put on our arms, we had to wait before being allowed to

wipe it off and apply anti-burn ointment.

'They asked what unit I wanted, medical sir, I said, then they gave me some tests. One was putting a draw handle together and the other was putting a washer back on a battery coupling, the simplest thing ever.

'Then I went in front of the officer, what would you like, medical corps sir. No, no, no he said you are mechanically minded.

'That's why I was put into the artillery.

Soon after being called up in 1942

I am very grateful to Tom for allowing me to use the following notes he has written, with the help of his daughter Carol, about his service during World War Two.

'I was posted to Chester 212 Light Anti-Aircraft (LAA) Training Regiment where I stayed for 10 weeks.

'I also learnt about the Bofors; eight men and one sergeant in a gun crew. I did not go to the firing camp because there were too many men to go. Instead, I had to scrub the gym floor at Satan Camp [Saighton Camp in Chester].

'After this training, I got my first leave, on return, I reported to Newmarket which was the HQ of 138 Light Anti-Aircraft Regiment. It was a holding regiment the reason being you could be posted anywhere, home or overseas.

'From there I was posted to 454 LAA battery which was at Duxford leading to a posting to A Troop 470 battery at a place called Warboys, which was a Lancaster Bomber Station.

'I was made a limber gunner, which meant I did not have to do Air Sentry during the day. There we had a book with pictures of aircraft that came out every month, I was good at aircraft recognition, so our gun crew used to win the prize of 60 free cigarettes!

'After all this training I was sent on a medical orderlies course in Rutland having been in St John's I was the ideal man to go on this course. In the meantime, the battery had moved to Newhaven on the south coast, so I had to follow them and reported back.

'After we had bombed the German dams in 1943, we were posted to Howden Dam in the Peak District. During the Second World War, the reservoir was used by pilots of the 617 Squadron for practising the low-level flights needed for Operation Chastise, the Dam Buster, due to its similarity to the German dams. We practised training our guns on them too.

'After this, I was promoted to Lance Bombardier. I had to give a training course as a medical orderly. Ladybower Reservoir was completed while we were there so we were withdrawn because Ladybower would have held the water if Howden had been bombed.

'After moving to different places, we went to a firing camp in Cumberland. As our bombardier had been taken away, I was promoted to Number One. I was the only number 1 on L3 gun team. We were fortunate on the clock and gate sight, we managed to hit the sleeve then we had what was called a technical shoot. The gunnery officer knocked out my sergeant, number seven and number four so the lads had to switch around and we hit the sleeve again, but firing at a sleeve being towed by a slow flying aircraft was quite easy, compared to what happened later.

'I was called to Battery HQ, twice, to be medical orderly as there were quite a few trying it on. I had to be medical orderly for the surrounding units. The second time the battery captain came up to me and asked 'Would you like to see some captured German aircraft? He took me because he did not know what they were.

'The Medical Captain came three times a week, in the meantime, I was my own boss. The second Medical Captain we had was a woman. The Battery Sergeant Major came to me and said I was going on an aircraft recognition instructor's course.

'The woman Medical Officer did not like it when I told her and said she would see the major – but it made no difference.

'My pay on joining the army was four shillings [twenty pence] a day, twentyeight shillings [one pound forty pence] a week. Then on promotion to Lance Bombardier I received an increase of one shilling and sixpence a day but, out of this, I sent seven shillings [thirty-five pence] a week to my mother.

'All through 1943-44 we were doing air sentry duty 24 hours a day. Out of our gun crew, the sergeant, bombardiers and cook never did air sentry duty so there was a lot of work for the remaining crew.

'While at Blackmoorfoot Dam near Huddersfield I had to go as a witness at courts marshal as one of our gunners was found asleep while on duty. We had all gone out for a drink, the gunner had more to drink, so he went on duty first with the instructions to wake me at 1245 hours unfortunately he didn't. He was sentenced to 56 days of detention.

'Also, while stationed at the dam one night, our gun crew was on air sentry duty when, around midnight, he heard a noise coming towards him. It was a plop, plop, plop getting near and nearer. He wondered what it could be. It turned out to be an old man with a wooden leg walking back home from the pub.

'A similar experience occurred to me. I was on air sentry on a brilliant moonlit night, not a sound to be heard. As I was walking up and down to keep awake, I heard a noise behind me. Spinning around to see what it was, but every time I turned it seemed OK, so I continued. I heard the noise again but still could not find where it was coming from. I stood still and found it was the cover of the Lewis gun flapping in the very slight breeze. This just shows how the imagination runs wild.

'I was reposted to 454 Battery A troop L3. From there we were sent to Essex between Walton-on-the-Naze and Frinton-on-Sea. All of a sudden, we were told we were going to Jaywick town (a bungalow town) in Clacton-on-Sea from there we went to Dover to learn how to fire rocket projectiles.

'This lasted a week with air raids every night being shelled by the cross-channel guns. We then returned to Clacton-on-Sea and trained on Bofors and rocket projectiles.

'I was then sent on a plotting course and the idea was for us to fire rockets at robot planes. One RAF officer, looking at aerial photographs, realised this was a little plane too small to be a regular plane – it was a robot plane. On the plotting course, they thought the robot planes would come in at speeds of over 600 mph, so we were going to have the radar set 10 miles in front of us so they could send in the height for us to fire rockets at them.

'One night, with a friend, I went for an evening out in Clacton. We spent the evening at the Odeon cinema. On coming out we went to the soldier's canteen on the front to have a tea and a wad (cake). As we left the sirens went, signalling an air raid. We started to make our way back to the camp at Jaywick town as the anti-aircraft started firing and flares were dropped by the enemy planes, then bombs. As we got halfway back to camp four more soldiers caught us up telling us that an incendiary bomb had landed through the roof of the cinema. By now a number of bombs had dropped which were quite near and all six of us dived for cover in the ditch. Quite a lot of these bombs never exploded, I often wondered even today if there are some of them still in the ground near Clacton. But we got back to camp safely. One of the chalets near us had taken a hit and the fire watchers were extinguishing the flames.

'We then moved to the Dover area just before the invasion on 6th June 1944. That day the sergeant and bombardier were away so I was in charge of the gun. There was not a lorry available for each gun the RASC [Royal Army Service Corps] would send lorries when needed. The night before the move orders were put up, I was the orderly sergeant and had to make sure everyone was up.

'On arriving in the Dover area, we were deployed near a village called Eastry. Not long after us, the Canadians moved in as part of the hoax that we were invading the Calais area. The area around Deal was all blocked off as if it was a holding place for tanks waiting to board ships.

'I was now transferred to A troop L1 because of too many aircraft recognition instructors in L3. From there for the next few weeks, we watched and heard the planes go over to the Calais area.

'Calais was thumped; you could feel the explosions on this side of the channel. On June 6th I had to report to battery HQ for a dental check, a two-mile walk, when I got there the news had just come through that the invasion had started in Normandy.

'On 12th June at 4 am our bombardier called us to man the gun. This was because these were the first flying bombs and no one in command was sure what they were. The next night, 14th June 1944, we were manning the gun in the evening on a 4-man crew when I noticed a motorbike coming up the road. This was one of our officers coming. We should have had a man on air sentry duty looking out for aircraft, but we were playing pitch and toss. I immediately got the binoculars and stood on the platform before he arrived. He then called the whole gun crew into the pit and told us that robot planes had been launched the previous night and we would now have to man, four men for twenty-four hours, every other day.

'The next night, 15th June, I was on duty with two other crew members as the sergeant and bombardier was sleeping in the pit just before 11.30. I reported to the sergeant that I would take the round off the tray, I was retiring for the night. On getting into the tent, I had just put my legs down in the blankets when they started firing at Dover. I immediately reported back to the gun pit, we were there all night.

'We kept having reports that flying bombs were being launched from France. One came over in the early hours (I can't remember the time) and we let fire for the first time. We fired 19 rounds but were situated in the wrong position. Later in the night, we fired at another, about 12 rounds, with no luck. Other guns had no better success.

'There were panic stations all around because there was a report going around that paratroopers were being dropped and the sergeant was informed to arm all the men not on duty with a rifle and 50 rounds of ammunition, and to bring the sten guns into the pit. This was a false alarm. The Canadian troops, we heard the next day, sent out patrols to look for the parachutes but shot one of their own. We changed over at six or seven in the morning so we could have a few hours' sleep. But we did not sleep long because the officers were coming round, and a full team was needed to man the gun. Meals were anyhow – as we had our own cook.

'In the afternoon, 2 pm, was the maintenance of the gun. After completing this we received orders that we would be moving immediately, complete with guns, tents and cook house. We were already waiting for the lorry to come; the troop officer came round in a 15cwt truck. He told me to get my small kit and go with him. There were six of us, one from each gun crew.

'He then took us to a crossroads and told us we should be meeting the rest of the troop here complete with guns later. We then made a right-hand turn down country lanes and when we got to a searchlight, we were told that this was the site of the first gun. I was the last one to receive a site and thought I would never find my way back that evening. We took two turns to the crossroads again where the troop was waiting for us.

'We had to set up the gun that night, part of the crew setting up the gun and the others organising tents. The next morning, at 6 am, we were having a cup of tea after being out all night when a flying bomb came followed by a Spitfire which promptly shot it down. We heard later that day that sixty soldiers had been killed when it crashed on a camp.

'This was not a successful [gun] site, so we moved again to the top of a hill where our tents were in some woods, it rained for days – we did not get undressed for a week just a pair of wellingtons to slip on. But it was realised by the powers that be that not every target coming in could be fired on by us. So, we got [more] information and were able to plot where the flying bomb was, we only got called for more realistic targets.

'We moved from the top of the hill so the barrage balloons could go there, we moved to the lower ground but this time with two guns per site. I remember one night I thought we had hit but the rain was setting off the shells just above our heads. We moved again to four guns per site. I was then informed I was going on a generator course for a few days; I waited at the gate for the lorry to pick me up. When it did come, I was told the course was cancelled and to go back to the site.

'Several incidents remain strongly in my mind like seeing a flying bomb coming over followed by a Spitfire, the Spitfire got very close and fired into the engine causing the flying bomb to drop like a stone with a big explosion nearby.

'We had two guns on one site and another flying bomb came over just as a thunderstorm started. We opened fire. Thought we had a hit – but hadn't. The heavy rain had prematurely exploded the fuses on some of our shells.

'Another night one crew was on 'relax', settling down on the gun cover, when all of a sudden, we could hear galloping hooves running towards us. Four horses at full gallop! There were panic stations, but the horses stopped just in time – the crews soon moved out of the way.

'In 1944 we moved back to the south coast and travelled through London seeing first-hand the damage that the flying bombs had caused. Whole streets were flattened. We returned to Folkestone on high ground but this time with the full battery of 12 guns. When we first started firing, we counted how many we shot down but now things had been organised we counted how many got through.

'When in action I saw flying bombs exploding in the air hit and coming down in flames. One went straight up in the air and then landed in the town of Hythe. One came down nose over tail and some came down spinning. One of them came in very low and our guns were at an angle of 70° when one of our shells hit the bomb overhead. I ducked my head behind the predictor and felt the blast around my legs. I turned and saw six feet of piping land nearby, but I never remembered hearing the explosion.

'The worst time was at night when we were off duty, trying to sleep in bell tents behind the guns. The firing of the guns would wake us up. One of us would look out to see which direction. If it was going left or right, we would relax but if it was coming straight on, we got ready to bail out. The residents of the coastal towns were not very pleased because they felt that they were being sacrificed for London. Remember when they landed, they were still bombs.

'From the beginning of September, fewer flying bombs were launched as our position in France strengthened and we moved back to Newhaven.

'Our gun site was near a housing complex. One day, two of our crew were looking through the telescopes on the predictor. When I looked to see what was holding their interest, they were looking at a half-dressed girl in a bedroom, one of the pleasures of air sentry.

'We then moved up the east coast and I went on leave. When I returned, there was no one to pick me up. I got a taxi to the site, he got me as close as possible but when I walked up to the field, they had all gone. I asked a neighbouring heavy battery who told me they had moved further down the coast and kindly took me down. It cost me £2/10 [two pounds and fifty pence] in taxi fares.

'This was an experimental site with four guns linked to one predictor – it did not work so we went non-operational. I was the NCO in charge of the picket. I had to man the phone all night long with rats all around, so I kept my feet on a chair off the floor. That night I heard my first V2 rocket land. At a meeting of the battery, we were told that the battery had been credited with shooting down 15 flying bombs.

'Our regiment was going to be disbanded so we moved down to Devon where all A1 men trained as infantrymen. The rest of us were posted

'One group was told they would be going to the Orkney Isles and the group I was in was told we were going to Aberdeen. But the truth came out that we were going to the Shetland Isles to 309 Heavy Anti-Aircraft Battery.

'It was at this time I experienced my longest train journey in Britain, it was October 1944. We set off from Barnstable on Saturday evening on a troop train we went through London, up to Carlisle and on to Glasgow. At Glasgow, our group changed trains and caught one to Aberdeen and we arrived at 1 am on Monday. We got off the train at Carlisle for sandwiches and to stretch our legs but otherwise, we slept on the train. Anyone who has travelled on a troop train during WW2 knows how atrocious the toilets became.

'From Aberdeen, we went by ship, which consisted of two ships and three armed trawlers, which took about 20 hours to get to the Shetland Isles. The weather was foul, most were seasick. On arriving in the Shetlands, we joined 309 heavy AA battery stationed on the Island of Bressay. 309 had a Number 10 predictor (the latest) and 584 radar set and 3.7 anti-aircraft guns. I became part of the control centre team; we released an equivalent number of A1 men to join the infantry.

'The weather in the Shetland Isles was wet and later snowy. Time off was a 24-hour pass to Lerwick. There were two half batteries, one in Lerwick and one on Bressay – this was later reduced to just a half battery on Bressay. We celebrated Christmas there, with a heavy snowfall, which meant that where we got our washing water all the pipes froze, so the water was short for washing, so a trip to Lerwick gave us a chance for a shower.

'I was guard commander one night and it was so cold we were issued with a rum ration. After Christmas, I was due for leave again so we set off, boarded the ship, had boat drill and after that experience, I retired immediately to the bunk I had been allocated.

'It was a very rough journey to Aberdeen. The small ship rolled, pitched and tossed all the way to Aberdeen. I arrived home in Loughborough on the 5th January 1945, my 21st birthday. My family got me a gold watch.

'On the way back to the Shetland Isles I experienced another very rough crossing as I slept on a mattress. The ship was an old Norwegian tramp and we had to board the ship according to our given number. At 1.00 am the ship sounded its siren because we had lost the escort and we put into Scapa Flow in the Orkneys. We waited there and then two destroyers took over the escort. We arrived in Lerwick at about 11 pm but were not allowed off till the next morning and after we had cleaned the decks from top to bottom.

'In May the war in Europe ended and I was lucky enough to be on a 24-hour pass in Loughborough when the celebrations took place. Then 309 Battery was moved to a place on the Thames estuary at Gillingham where we got special long-range guns. This was experimental equipment aimed at giving some defence against the V2s.

'The brigadier was coming to see how the new equipment was working but those not directly involved were detailed off to cut the long grass. I scythed a cable which was from the radar set to the control room. I got a shock in more ways than one.

'I timidly went down to the control centre and told an officer. He just laughed and told me to go to the radar sergeant who sorted it with black tape.

'I was not aware of the atomic bombs but had heard people talking about them when on leave and the next day one was dropped. This brought the end of the war against Japan. We celebrated VJ day with crowds of people in Gillingham for hours.

With VJ Day World War Two may have been over, but as Tom was about to find out his military service was not. Tom had spent his entire war service in Great Britain, but that was about to change.

'All troops had an age and service group, given my age and service group I was 50, so I was not expecting an immediate discharge. As 309 Battery was being disbanded, I was put on a draft to go to Egypt.

'I had a 14-day leave pass and I had to break the news to the family I was to go abroad. I was determined not to let my sisters go to the station with me as they had done when I was called up in 1942.

'I had to report to the Grand Hotel at Clacton where we were processed and went by train to Newhaven where we caught a ship to Dieppe. From Tuesday night, at about 2 am, we travelled till 11 am Thursday to get to Toulon. The journey was uncomfortable. There were six to a compartment and we slept two on the seats, two on the luggage racks and two on the floor. It was a bad night – every time you wanted to turn you had to nudge your mate to turn too. The next night I had the seat.

'One of our party, Bill Molyneaux, had been a runner for the French Resistance. At a food stop, where we were served by French women, one made a remark about his premature baldness. She was very surprised when he was able to reply in the local dialect.

'From Toulon, we sailed on a French liner called the Champollion landing at Alexandria about 3 days later. The officers had the staterooms, the ranks slept in hammocks. We caught a train down to Cairo (Almarza), a massive camp. We went there until posted out to a unit.

'I was posted to the Middle East School of Artillery and put in a range battery which did the firing for the technical people. In range battery, it was said I would make a good signaller – when I asked why they referred to the original tests in 1942 as I joined up.

'Then we had a Commandant inspection one morning. We had our beds outside, waiting for attention, he probably noticed that my flaming brigade badge was worn due to continued polishing. He asked what I was doing, and I said signalling, but I would sooner be on the guns. I looked out of the corner of my eye and there were the RSM and Battery Sergeant Major. I thought no more about it. After Taffy, the runner, came and asked me to report to the RSM's office. I duly did.

'The RSM asked me if I would like to be his clerk or the mail orderly, I chose mail orderly – a popular job. I went into the tent and who had just moved in but Geoff Holden, which was the start of a long friendship. The current mail orderly was being demobbed. I got my stripe back and was in the office one afternoon and I was invited to try to type. I looked at this bloke on my right, a beanpole with a big nose and glasses, a real drip. He turned out to become one of my best mates, Gerald Sherlock.

'I used to collect the mail every day and make sure that it went out right. It was a very interesting time – mail could be infrequent, I was always prepared to collect mail, send parcels and record people coming in.

'I always knew when RSM Brown, Topper Brown, was in a good mood because he said 'Good Morning Carter' rather than bombardier. He often told me to put my hat on and be an escort, an interesting job. We worked in the morning and two hours at night.

1945 in Egypt

'If I needed to go to the Mail PO in Almarza I just had to ring for transport.

'We met two young Egyptian lads. The Egyptians ran the canteen and laundry and Mustapha was under the illusion that the Egyptians had bought all our equipment.

'I had a great time in Egypt and made many lifelong friends including Geoff Holden, Ged Sherlock, Wally Harrison and Norman Worsman.

'Other names are strong in my memory Dusty Miller, Smudgy Smith, Bill Molyneaux, Geoff Hill and a young Scot called Jock. I even got a new name myself – Nick (after Nick Carter, the fictional detective) and I am still called this by my army mates.

'There was some entertainment in the camp, a cinema and a boxing ring, we also entertained ourselves with singing, drinking and larking around. I also got a chance of sightseeing and visited the pyramids at Giza and Saqqara. I went inside the Great Pyramid to see the King's Chamber and got to see the step pyramid and the temple of the sacred bulls.

'In November 1946 Geoff and Ged went home on leave and The School of Artillery left the camp and moved to Palestine, just north of Haifa. We spent Christmas 1946 there and I hoped to go to Bethlehem on Christmas Eve, but too many wanted to go.

'In January 1947 I had a month's leave and returned home. One of my mates never got called up, he worked at Morris as a draughtsman, I met up with him that leave, that is how I met Jean Wartnaby, she worked at Morris.

'I expected to return to Palestine but, just before the end of my leave, I received a telegram saying I was reverting to home establishment and had to report to Woolwich Arsenal.

'On 5th May 1947 I left the army, I went to get my civilian clothes and was demobbed.

Tom returned to his hometown of Loughborough after his demob, but as he said to me, he knew life would be different.

'I went back to my old job, but didn't stay long, my sisters were still at Morris, so I got a job there.

'Then on Saturday 6th June 1948 Jean and I got married at Loughborough Emmanuel Church, with Geoff Holden attending the ceremony.

'Soon I remember going on a three-day week, I handed my notice in and went to The Brush and stayed there until I retired, and I enjoyed it.

'When I first started, I worked in the motor shop where they were making electric motors for diesel engines, we had to make so many a week. But then I transferred to be an inspector where I checked all the motors at despatch, I did not work in an office.

Tom admitted his army service helped him as an inspector acknowledging, that he would not stand for any rubbish or fooling, soon gaining a reputation that it had to be right, every time.

Tom and Jean would have two children, Carol and David, but Tom's life changed massively in the summer of 1976. Both children were now in their late teens, Carol had just graduated, and David was still at university.

'I had been to the hospital when I got home Jean said she was going to bed, she suffered from migraines, so she went to bed. I stayed down. Later I walked into the bathroom, she was flat on the floor I turned her over and tried to resuscitate her. That was a shock.

After losing Jean so suddenly, Tom returned to one of his boyhood passions, singing. This time with The Loughborough Male Voice Choir along with other singing groups. Tom admitted this gave him company and he was always willing to help with productions.

'I can always remember going on stage at the town hall, at the end of the show I was on stage and had to stamp my foot and shout 'Only in the Name of France.' When I met the sound manager, he said you don't need a microphone.

Tom also attended the Solo Club, a club for single, bereaved people, where he met Beryl and with time, they were to get married. Tom and Beryl were very happy together, Tom was still appearing in shows and Beryl worked behind the scenes. Soon after marrying, Tom and Beryl moved to her house in nearby East Leake.

With time they moved back into Loughborough. Sadly, Beryl's health started failing with the onset of dementia, soon she moved into a care home but sadly passed away in the spring of 2021. Since losing Beryl, Tom has lived alone, but he is still busy with his drawing and keeps himself very active and mobile.

Before I bid my farewell to Tom, I asked him what he puts down to his long and healthy life, given he is still so active in his late nineties.

'I was born into a big family, we weren't rich, you managed, I did the same in the war when you did what you could for your country, to me your country comes first. You have to get on with what you have got.

A few weeks after meeting Tom his family told me that he had passed away peacefully in his sleep following a short illness. But were still determined that his story should be told.

Arthur Perkins
Royal Inniskilling Fusiliers

I caught up with Arthur and his wife Tonie at home close to the centre of Nottingham, both have been lifelong residents of the city and they were busy counting down the days to Arthur's one-hundredth birthday, which was fast approaching.

Arthur was christened William Arthur Perkins, as was his father and in turn, his father before him. His grandfather was always known as William and his father was Bill, so it is of little surprise that he became Arthur as a young child. Born in Deptford Street, Bulwell on 15th January 1923 Arthur has strayed little from the city except for his service during World War Two.

The only child of Ada and Bill Perkins, who was known as '*Bill the Borer*' due to his occupation as a coal miner. Bill worked for forty years at Bestwood Colliery, in its day, Bestwood was one of the most successful coal mines in the county's coalfield, at its peak employing over two thousand men, before closing in 1967.

Arthur remembers his mother, Ada, working as a dyer on Station Street in Nottingham, when she was at work Arthur would spend the day with his grandmother, often arriving at seven in the morning.

Arthur's father Bill had a noticeably short military career in World War One with the Coldstream Guards; it lasted just one day in 1916, as he was sent home immediately after joining. His career in the coal industry was seen as far more valuable than any military service.

'I had a lot of uncles growing up, my grandma on my mother's side had fifteen children. My uncle Bill served in World War One and he was lucky to be alive, he always told us the same tale. He was injured and fell into a shell hole in No Man's Land, he was still laying there when the Germans came past, there were about six or seven of them and they stopped and looked at him as one of the Germans picked his rifle up to shoot him. Then their officer knocked it out of his hand saying we don't shoot injured people. He would always tell us that tale and that's why he came back alive, I think he was in The Sherwood Foresters, the local regiment.

'My other uncle, my mother's eldest brother was also called Arthur. Arthur Anthony, he was a policeman, he joined about 1920, he was in Basford one night and got attacked by five yobs, he was only twenty 'cos he had not had his twenty-first birthday. He never did a day's work after that in the police, he was on full-time sick and died soon after he turned ninety.

Arthur went to Albert Street School, Highbury Vale, which was demolished many years ago. He was a keen sportsman at school playing both football and cricket, he carried on playing cricket after school and played for several teams including Basford and Raleigh, he also played against the Taverners where he remembers scoring over twenty runs.

Then as he got older Arthur became a cricket umpire, one particularly proud moment was to umpire on the country ground at Trent Bridge during a match of Notts Colts, Arthur retired from cricket umpiring in the late 1970s.

'In 1937, I think 27th September a Tuesday night. I had a decent bike and I went to my cousin Harry, 'Shall we have a bike ride' he answered no I am cleaning my bike. Alright, Harry, I'll clean mine then, I started cleaning mine, I turned it upside down and got a piece of rag on my finger with some stuff on it, then I turned the chain, my finger went around the cog.

I went into my aunties and said look what I have done when winding the chain around, she fainted. We fetched a cousin of ours, Tede [her name was Edith, but always known as Tede] who was living with my grandma, she came as she had some experience in first aid, she bought my dad and we jumped on the tram and went to the hospital. The old

General Hospital at the top of Mount Street, we sat there, it was about eight when we got there, I know it was eleven when they fetched me in the operating room.

'I put my arm out and didn't feel anything, the surgeon looked up, and said, 'Umm twenty minutes not a bad job.' He had finished with me in twenty minutes and took my finger off. He said to my dad, we could have saved it, but the finger would have been straight all his life and it would have been no good to him, so it is better as it is.

Little did Arthur know at that time, those twenty minutes in losing his finger, the index finger on his right hand, would have a profound effect on his life in future years.

'My first job was working at Bulwell Dyers, where I was presented with half a crown [twelve and a half pence] a week, then I got a job in Ashwells Textiles in New Basford. It was a ladies hosiery factory, I was turning, which was taking the items off the press as the bloke in charge was putting them in the press, once I took them off I would fold them up the best I could.

'Then in 1939 I started at Players, 13th September 1939, ten days after the war started, I worked on the top floor taking stuff down to the warehouse ready for distribution. They turned out about a million and quarter cigarettes a day, I moved thirty boxes, about 30,000 cigarettes at a time.

'When I got to eighteen, I was given twenty-five cigarettes every week, that started me smoking, I smoked until 1976, then I went into hospital. They found I was diabetic, really diabetic, she said no smoking before your op, it was the matron she was a right so and so, a proper old matron. The operation is a week on Friday, I said that means, I haven't got a cigarette till a week on Friday. No, no she said you are not to smoke until then.

I said, oh dear and took some Senior Service from my pocket and chucked them on her desk, saying 'Well if I can't smoke them, you smoke them.' I haven't had one since.

On 27th January 1942, Arthur was conscripted into the Army when he received his call-up letter.

'It was a Wednesday I think, on the Friday or the Saturday I was in Northern Ireland as I was put in the Inniskilling Fusiliers, it was not my choice to join them it was where I was posted on conscription. My number was 6985688. There were quite a few different people, I remember a lot of Londoners, one went out and got wood then come back so we had a decent fire 'cos it was damn cold. I ended up at 25 ITC in Northern Ireland in Omagh, County Tyrone.

The only photograph that Arthur has in his uniform

Arthur did all his basic military training in Northern Ireland, leaving in late May or June 1942 when he was posted to 1st Battalion Royal Irish Fusiliers, initially to Cumnock in Scotland where King George VI visited the battalion. They then moved to the New Forest, Hampshire, at Burley in preparation for the North Africa campaign.

'The Sergeant Major took us all to the rifle range, it was the first time I had fired a rifle and I could not hit the target. I was picked out by the Sergeant Major who took me on my own. He watched everything I did, but I still could not hit the target. He said 'You're no good to us, I am not bothered about you, but you can't fire a rifle to save your mates, you are hopeless.

It was Arthur's missing finger that caused the problem. He could not hold the rifle firmly enough and was only just able to fire the rifle. Arthur was medically downgraded and sent back to Belfast, it was now November 1942. In a matter of days, his battalion was on route to North Africa.

'That finger saved my life, the battalion was getting ready to go to North Africa and I lost a lot of mates, there were quite a few who did not get back. On returning to Northern Ireland, I had two or three interviews with different people trying to find out what I could do, they tried me as a batman for an officer – But didn't really suit.

One story that Arthur remembered of his time back in Northern Ireland involved a stray dog that had been around the barracks.

> 'I threw it a bit of my dinner, after that it would not leave me. It was a collie cross dog that was patient, very good and did everything I told him. If I told him to sit, he would, so I bought him home. It was the train to Larne, a ferry to Stranraer then a train to Derby and a bus from Derby to Nottingham which dropped me at Basford crossings, it was then one of the old trams. The inspector said upstairs with the dog and followed me, then said 'You can travel free [Arthur was in uniform] but it's a penny for the dog.

The dog was named Paddy, he stayed with Arthur's parents then later, after the war, with Arthur, becoming a much-loved family pet.

> 'I was then sent to Aldershot, a first aid place where you learnt all about first aid, I had three or four weeks there, then I trained as a medical orderly which lasted a good while.

> 'Then I was told I was being transferred to 9/10 Dock Operating Company, a DOC. This was now late 1943 and I transferred to the Royal Engineers.

After serving with DOC in several locations including Liverpool, Arthur arrived at Aveley on the River Thames, east of London. Surprisingly, Arthur was not employed for his recent qualifications, as a Medical Orderly, but as part of the labouring gangs loading the ships.

> 'While at Aveley, we were made the number one petrol port, so we loaded nothing but petrol, that's when the V1 Doodle Bugs started to come over. So, we had five thousand tons of petrol underneath us in one ship, we had got three ships as Doodle Bugs were flying over the top. They missed our ships but one hit other ships in Royal Albert Dock with the loss of many lives.

> 'After this, I was transferred to Dover, stationed in Dover castle, still loading ships but now different things, ammunition, food, all sorts of things. I realised afterwards it was for the [D Day} invasion as it was the beginning of 1944, February or March time.

Then in February 1946, he was posted to North Africa, first at Port Said, then Alexandria and finally Port Tawfik where he oversaw the Medical Inspection Rooms.

'I had four MI Rooms, plus a doctor, he was only about five foot tall he was Dutch, but a very good doctor. I slept in the MI room and was excused from all parades, even pay parades, my money was bought for me, as I was on duty 24 hours a day. Between me and the doctor we had four different battalions to go to, we would go around and give them the needle for TABT and TT. I would give them the TT, leave the needle in their arm and the doctor would give them the TABT.

'Then in November 1946, I came back. They reckoned up my leave that I should have had, that leave finished on 27th January 1947, five years to the day since I was called up.

I asked Arthur what his thoughts were after being demobbed and moving back to Nottingham.

'Sometimes it was enjoyable at other times it wasn't, I probably would not have missed it, because it was an eye opener, to meet and see how other people lived. I remember three good friends while in England and went to Egypt with them, we kept each other company. One was called Rhodes, who we called Dusty; Dusty Rhodes, he was about ten years older than me. Another one was Billy Streets and the third one was Johnny Dale who was much younger than me. They are the only three I can remember that didn't get killed, I never met them again or spoke to them, somehow we never swapped addresses.

In the early spring of 1947, back to *'civvy street'* in Nottingham, Arthur went back to Players asking for his old job.

'I went in front of a board who said, 'I am sorry, but you started work here after the war started, if you had started before the war, we would have taken you back, but because you started on 13th September, we can't employ you. So, I did not get employed there and lost my job, so I had to find a bit of a job which was building, jobbing building. I was there until September when I tried the pit and went down the pit as a bricklayer.

Arthur was now married, meeting his first wife before he joined up, they married while he was in the army in 1943 but sadly separated in the early

1970s. They had a son, Robert, born just before Christmas 1944, who sadly passed away shortly before I met Arthur.

> 'I stayed down the pit until 1962 when I had an accident to my ankle, then I went long distance driving for a start, then in 1969 I went to Raleigh as a security guard. Where I worked for thirteen years before being made redundant, that's where I met this lady [pointing to his second wife - Tonie] and we got married in 1972.

In marrying Tonie, Arthur gained two children, Mark and Penny, both aged younger than ten, who called him *'pop'* for years and regarded Arthur as their father growing up. Mark joined the Royal Navy and saw service in the South Atlantic during the Falklands War in 1982.

> 'After being made redundant I went working for Manpower Services, they would send me twenty-four men and I was teaching them different building skills, bricklaying, joinery and painting. I had one lad who made a good painter. We did a lot of repairs and work on local churches; the church would buy the material and we provided the labour. I was there four years and then retired.

Arthur finally retired from work in 1988 aged sixty-five, but it was not a time to put his feet up, after a busy and active life, much of it helping other people, he continued helping local disadvantaged people along with charity work.

Following retirement Arthur also worked as a volunteer driver taking young children to foster care, which he did until he was seventy, only stopping as he was no longer allowed to drive given his age. As Tonie commented, Arthur was never happier than when he was helping somebody.

> 'I have always been the same if someone wants help I would do it, I get frustrated now 'cos I can't do it the same.

Today both Arthur and Tonie are retired, they will soon have been married for fifty years. Both are still fully supportive and active in their church, which they say is about its community, rather than its religion. The two of them have lived in the same house since 1975, but looking to the future they are now considering a move to be closer to their daughter in the north of England.

Val Hilton
Auxiliary Territorial Service

I met with Val, along with her son Leigh, dodging rain showers on a sunny afternoon at her residential care home on the Derbyshire - Staffordshire border. Sadly, Val's dementia prevented any interview with her; but it was Leigh who told me; *'We do have Val's story.'*

In 2008 Val recorded much of her life story on an audio recorder, the recording starts; 'I have recorded some details of my life - In case my sons are interested ...' So, this is very much Val's story, even if told over a decade ago, with the gaps filled in by her family.

Valerie, or as she has always been known, Val, is the only child of Lionel Pierce and Grace Tulk, she was born on 28th October 1925, in a nursing home at Headingly, Leeds. Her father Lionel was born in Hastings, one of four boys and Grace was a native of Sherborne, Dorset. When Val was born her father, Lionel, was an apprentice engineer, later joining the Merchant Navy, but sadly aged just thirty-one contracted double pneumonia and died.

In 1932, Val's mother, Grace, met Les Pawson, they would be together for the next twenty-five years. Les was a highly skilled and gifted violinist, playing in Hastings at The White Rock Pavilion along with various other seaside resorts, at a time when the seaside holiday was in its glory days. In addition to this, he was part of a London orchestra, plus the Halle Orchestra in Manchester. Grace and Les would go on to have a daughter, Jennifer, who was born on 19th December 1939 in Hastings.

Until she was seven Val, lived in the family home at Hastings, where she admitted to being very happy. But, after Grace met Les, she led a very nomadic lifestyle, it was not unusual for her to stay in rooms where Les was playing or teaching the violin, just sitting waiting for him.   For Val, it was not a happy time, but Val was able to go and stay with her grandmother, Grace's mother, known as Margaret.

Not much is known about Margaret, but I am thankful to Val's family for the following. In 1901 Margaret, aged twenty-three had moved to North Road, Sherborne in Dorset to work as a cook and housekeeper for Mr Edward Fooks, a solicitor and Justice of the Peace. About this time, she met Frank Tulk, a mason's labourer, who was living in the next street, the following summer, believed to be August 1902, they were married, and moved to Acreman Street, Sherborne. They had four children; Cyril the eldest was born the year after they married and Grace was born in 1906, later Olive and Doris arrived.

Val always spoke of her grandmother, Margaret, as a kind and loving lady, but this could still be a lonely time for her as a child. Add to this her lifestyle made schooling a challenge for Val, she attended schools in Hastings, Whitby and Frome.

Les was not called up for military service during World War Two, but he did carry out several administrative roles in support of the war effort. Then going on to join the Entertainments National Service Association, often better known as ENSA, which was established at the outbreak of war to entertain the armed forces and functioned as part of the NAAFI.

Grace joined the Auxiliary Territorial Service, or the ATS, in London soon after the outbreak of war in 1939. At this time both Val and Jen were being cared for by their grandmother, Margaret, who was now living in Frome. Val and Jen lived with their grandmother as evacuees, as part of Operation Pied Piper.

Operation Pied Piper was the evacuation of civilians during the Second World War. The objective was to shield people, especially children, from the risks of bombing, by moving them to areas at less risk of bombing, usually rural communities.

The operation began at 5.00 am on the morning of 1st September 1939, as the war started. More than three and a half million, some seven per cent of the population, became evacuees during the war, but some parents refused to send their children as reports emerged of children being ill-treated. It was not unusual for city children to be sent to the country to find better living conditions, but equally, children could come from houses with indoor bathrooms to cottages with no running water, gas or electricity. For some children, the end of the war stopped the confusion and fear they suffered during years of separation. But in other cases, it was a massive upheaval, feeling they were being forced to return to cities and families they barely remembered and a lifestyle they had forgotten.

Grace was able to leave the ATS after just twelve months of service as she had a child, Jen, under school age. After she resigned Grace returned to Frome and was reunited with both Val and Jen. Val was now aged fourteen and finishing school, she soon started work at a local factory making engine parts, where she was employed in the office. Additionally, Val studied in the evenings, at Frome School of Art, learning book-keeping and shorthand.

With the war still raging in Europe, Val, aged just seventeen applied to both the Royal Navy and the Royal Air Force, both had vacancies for cooks and orderlies, which Val decided was not for her. So, she followed her mother and joined the ATS, soon qualifying as a driver and spent the rest of the war driving heavy trucks and lorries wherever the ATS needed them.

I cannot help but think, as I listened to Val's story, that this could be unique. Both mother and daughter served in the ATS during World War Two; maybe not at the same time, but between them they served for much of the war.

During World War Two, The Auxiliary Territorial Service, often known as the ATS, was the women's branch of the Army, it was formed before the outbreak of war in September 1938 and disbanded as it merged into the Women's Royal Army Corps in February 1949. The ATS had its foundations in the Women's Auxiliary Army Corps (WAAC) formed in the latter part of the First World War, when over 17,000 of its volunteer members served overseas,

Soon after VE Day, as the war in Europe finished in 1945, Val was posted as a staff-car driver for a Lieutenant Colonel. With the posting she moved

Val photographed in 1946 whist serving in the ATS.
The photograph was taken by a German POW at Tewkesbury, during a visit to
the POW Camp by a RASC Colonel when Val was his driver

and was stationed in Leeds. She clearly remembers one occasion when she was slowly driving onto a parade ground, where the Lieutenant Colonel was to inspect the assembled troops when the back wheel came off her car and rolled past them. The car came to a grinding halt, with the wheel crossing the parade ground in front of them. Not impressed, the Colonel did not speak to Val for a week.

Val was demobbed from the ATS in York, then shortly afterwards moved to London to study at secretarial college, it was a chance to brush up on her shorthand and typing skills, which had been neglected during the war.

Val enjoyed her time in London, attending theatres and ballet. But after eighteen months, she moved to Buxton in Derbyshire to be with her mum Grace, Les and Jennifer as Val took a job with the Tax Office in Buxton.

In 1948, Val met Harold Hilton, who had served in the war as a navigator in India, with the Royal Air Force as a Sergeant. Harold joined the tax office as a student, whilst studying to be a teacher at St. Peter's Teacher Training College at Saltley in Birmingham, they were engaged within a year and married on 11th April 1950. They initially lived in a flat in Buxton and later at a house in Dove Holes.

After finishing college Harold started teaching at Whaley Bridge school, then in 1961 successfully applied for the post of headmaster at Aston-on-Trent Primary School, in South Derbyshire, where he worked for the next twenty-two years until his retirement aged sixty. Harold and Val would have two sons, Michael was born in 1951 and Leigh in 1953.

During this time Val worked as a secretary at ICI, then at Rolls Royce and finally with The Ministry of Agriculture, from where she retired. Harold & Val enjoyed ten years of happy retirement together, taking holidays at Clacton, Frinton, Southport & Frome. This was followed by several holidays abroad including Australia, where Harold's younger sister Margaret lived with her husband Dennis, who had emigrated in the early 1960s on the Assisted Passage Migration Scheme.

With time Harold's failing health persuaded them to move to a bungalow in Aston-on-Trent, it was 1991. At the same time, Val was diagnosed with a muscular and nervous disorder, which left her with bouts of extreme tiredness. To add to their misfortunes, soon after this Val's mother, Grace, had a stroke. Grace moved to a warden-controlled bungalow, situated in the next village, but eventually needed to move into a nursing home, Grace sadly passed away in 1996, aged ninety. During this time Harold became seriously ill and passed away just a year later in 1997, aged just seventy-four, as Leigh said to me, an exceptionally fine man who we all still miss today.

Val & Harold's two sons Michael & Leigh both led successful careers, Michael as a Civil Engineer & Project Manager and Leigh as a Senior Auditor. Today both are happily married with four children between them and five grandchildren.

Val was able to remain in her bungalow at Aston-on-Trent until 2015, living by herself, but following a fall and increasing symptoms of dementia she moved into a nearby Residential Care Home. Today her family visit regularly, but despite being frail, she is still in reasonable health.

Ken Hoddy
The Rifle Brigade

I met Ken living at home in Nottinghamshire, he still had the mannerism and bearing of the soldier he was some seventy years ago, he is still regularly active and busy, despite being in his mid-nineties.

'I was born on 23 September 1927 in Saltaire, near Bradford, it had one of the largest woollen mills in Europe, Salts Mill. My father was an engineer, he worked at a place called Butterfield making big tanks, water tanks and was an amateur boxer, while my mother worked at Salts Mill.

'Talking of boxing, by all accounts my father went to the fairground, his friends got him up and he knocked this bloke down in two or three seconds and became renowned as a boxer and he got a great big cup. A fantastic cup and I always remember my mother having an argument with him saying you can only hit women, he got this cup and smashed it, the dustbin men mended it and had it in the front of their van for years.

'My dad's name was Herbert, Herbert Hoddy and my mum was Beatrice Helen, but was always called Betty, which is why my sister was called Betty.

'My grandparents lived in the area, my grandfather was a bargee on the Leeds and Liverpool Canal, they had three sons and one daughter, which was my mother. They lived in a place in Shipley, my grandma had two houses in Regents Street in Saltaire and we lived in one of them.

'As I said my grandfather was a bargee for the mill before the war, he went on to become an RSM in World War One, in the West Riding Regiment and

he got the MM [Military Medal] his name was Wright, Jim Wright. I never saw his [medal] citation, so I don't know what it was for. He was quite fit and survived the war, after he came out his wife died, he married again and lived in the alms houses at Salts Mill.

'I hated school; I got the cane every Friday for spelling. I realised, after being a teacher for many years, it was the teacher's fault, not the kid's fault. But unfortunately, because of the war, they put all the teachers that had retired back into the schools, and they had little idea of teaching, it was ruled by the cane. I have now been, for a long time, a mature student and that caused me some hard work.

'But at school, I excelled in boxing, two teachers were boxing fanatics, I went to Leeds and got a medal for the best loser, I won it the next year, and I went on to become the West Riding Flyweight Champion.

It was just after Ken's twelfth birthday that the Second World War started, I asked him if he could remember the outbreak of war or the announcement on the BBC.

'One of the first things I remember was my father and my mother talking in a whisper, writing on an envelope. I don't know what they were doing, but the next day, when I came from school, I was laying the fire, then all of a sudden, my father came in, my father was a territorial he had served with them for about four years. He came in and he said, I've got an important job for you, take this envelope and go down to the mill and get your mother.

'So, I went down to the mill as fast as I could, the gate man said to go into that door there. That door was the weaving shed with 300 looms going at full blast, I couldn't hear a thing. The over-looker came forward and said what do you want, I give him this envelope and he dashed away. My mother came and we went to the house.

'When we got there, my dad was putting his puttees on and my mother started filling his kit bag, then we went down to Green Lane Barracks, I was very proud to carry my father's kit bag.

'All the territorials were assembling there, and there were hundreds of families there all around waiting to see what happened. Then the buses started coming, we were waiting three hours for my father to come out. I

suppose they were waiting for orders. I was quite proud when I saw my father march out with a Lewis Gun on his shoulder. He beckoned me to the bus and said, 'You're the man of the house now Ken, look after your mother and sister'.

'I was quite proud, as I took my mother and sister home. Then I found every father had gone to war with the front door key of the house.

'I didn't know where he was going or when he was coming back. But he went to a place called Driffield and set up a camp there. He was with the artillery, light Ack Ack.

'I started work at 14, I finish school Friday and I went to Salts Mill the next morning. When I got there, I had to go through an initiation. This was standard those days, I went into the spinning looms [shed] and these women debagged me and put me in a stroll skip and I ended up going up and down all morning. I was shouting for help, but I was strapped in this skip, and then at dinnertime, I could hear all these women says he's in a skip and they all got around this skip and they pulled me out. I could hear one woman say he is a big boy, but I was very tall for my age at that time.

'I joined the Army Cadets, and I was boxing for the West Riding, I was doing all right, and they selected me to go to Aldershot on a PT course. I had never been out of Shipley and Saltaire and I had to go to Aldershot. I got on a train at Bradford Forster Square and went to King's Cross and when I got to King's Cross there was an air raid on.

'So, I couldn't go on the underground, I asked a policeman, and he said to follow the crowd they're going over to Waterloo. I followed the crowd and went over to Waterloo, it was the first time I saw a V1, right over Leicester Square.

'I passed as a PT Instructor, the reason for this was, people joining the army at that time were so unfit because they were on rations and it took a long time to get them up to standard again, health-wise. So, they thought it would a clever idea to train instructors in PT to train the Army Cadets in PT and get them fit before they volunteered for the army.

'I was just fifteen I had left school the year before.

Ken admits that he excelled in the Army Cadets, which in turn gave him a massive advantage when he enlisted in September 1944.

'I couldn't get in the army quick enough. I joined up and saw someone in The Rifle Brigade and thought, I fancy that, or the Paras, so I went to the recruiting office. They said it would be easier to get into the Paras from The Rifle Brigade. So, I joined The Rifle Brigade.

'When I joined up, I went to York, to Fulford Barracks, and I excelled in the army because I had been in the Army Cadets, shooting, field craft, everything and I came top in most things. I was asked then to go on an advanced course for mechanised infantry at Ranby Camp, it's a prison now – well it was a prison then.

'So, I went to Ranby camp, I was picked up by the duty vehicle at the station and went to the guardroom the provost sergeant came out and said. 'Are you for this advanced course, well believe it or not there is a bloke just come in a chauffeur driven car, he is in the guard room at the moment, waiting for you; he doesn't half talk posh.' I think he was waiting for a place in Sandhurst. So, he introduced me to this bloke; he hadn't got a bloody clue.

'We went down and filled his pally ass, not too much just lightly, then we went into the hut. Where the stove was in the middle, everyone had their beds near, we had to have a bed at the end.

'He said, what do we do now, I said there are two bunks and first, we will toss up for who has the bottom bunk, I got the bottom bunk. I thought all my Christmases had come at once. Until in the middle of the night, I found he was a bed wetter.

'A few days later we were told it was going to be VE Day. Ranby Camp had a small parade square, and we had troops coming back [from the war]. Our screaming skull, the RSM, was at his best, he had a job to get them all closed in, he was screaming and shouting. Around the square is a three-foot wall, which separated the gym.

'So, we paraded and lined up when the Commanding Officer, Vic Turner VC, and his Adjutant were coming up on the square. The RSM had a strange mannerism of walking backwards when he was giving his order of command, which he shouldn't, but he always walked backwards with a pace stick under his arm, and he fell over the gym wall. He went straight

over and a thousand and one of us saw it, he never got up. I can hear the laughter and words now, I hope he hasn't hurt himself, or words to that effect. It was hilarious the place was in an uproar, I heard die you bastard. He still never got up, someone said to get a medic they loaded him on a stretcher and took him away.

'The adjutant had to sort out the parade, calling stop this shouting and the CO came on the parade and announced he was having an extra pay parade, and this is a London Regiment, The Rifles, and I don't want anyone to go to London. We got our pay, then he said there would be passion wagons arranged that evening and you are going down to Retford, as they are having some celebrations.

'I got on the passion wagon went into town, the square in Retford had big pebbles, like cobblestones and we were dancing, seeing who could make the most sparks fly off their ammo boots, sparks were flying all over the place.

'It was VE Night. That night I met the wife, I would be with her for sixty-four years.

Ken spoke about Vic Turner VC, his CO at the VE Day pay parade. This was Lieutenant Colonel Victor Buller Turner VC, CVO. Lieutenant Colonel Turner was awarded the Victoria Cross (VC) during the Battle of El Alamein in October 1942, when he was commanding a battalion of The Rifle Brigade.

But he is somewhat unique because his older brother, Alexander, was also awarded a VC, during the First World War at the Battle of Loos.

Alexander Buller Turner was a twenty-two-year-old Second Lieutenant, serving in the Royal Berkshire Regiment when he was awarded the VC on 28 September 1915, sadly he died of injuries he sustained in the action just a couple of days later.

Together they are part of a very select group of Victoria Cross recipients, only four pairs of brothers - including the Turner brothers, have been awarded the VC. But they are the only brothers to have received a VC in World War One and World War Two.

'Betty, my younger sister, joined the ATS when she could. She worked in

the mill till she was able to go into the ATS.

'I was at Aldershot at that time, and I went up to Guildford where she was in training and her sergeant let us out to go for a cup of coffee. I got pulled up with the Red Caps because she was linking arms with me.

'My Sister worked at a scientific place, she did about three or four years in the army, ATS. Later she married a city policeman, in the dark days of the Krays, I understand one of the Kray

Ken's sister Betty, in ATS Uniform

henchmen shot his sergeant. My sister died about five years ago.

Remembering that Ken was thinking of joining the Parachute Regiment, which had only been formed a couple of years before, I asked him if he was disappointed in not joining them.

'When I got to the battalion I was still down for the Paras and I went from the battalion to Aldershot for the course, then at Upper Heyford to do my jumps. The idea was in the regiment they were going to have a platoon of paratroopers which could go in advance and set up a beachhead and things like that. Then every six months you had to go back and take your jumps to keep your jump pay.

'I was the youngest sergeant in the regiment for about six months and that caused me a lot of problems, in that the majority were elderly sergeants and I got every dirty job you could get.

'I remember Operation Woodpecker in the Harz Mountains [in Germany]. When we had no wood and all the lads went into the Harz Mountains chopping down trees, they called timber - Another one hundred lousy doors for England, home and glory.

Ken's in Uniform about 1947

'The wood was sent to England, it was that cold winter of 1947, we would pull the trees out with horses or half-tracks.

Operation Woodpecker was something I had not heard of previously, but after World War Two there was a dire shortage of timber for house building and construction across the country.

The government's answer was to cut down trees in Germany and ship the timber to Great Britain, using the Army based in Germany as the workforce.

Four sites were found, in Germany, for the work including Goslar, on the northern slopes of the Harz Mountains, where Ken supervised the cutting of trees. Some 40,000 tons of timber, sufficient for 7,000 homes, had been shipped by the end of March 1947.

However, Operation Woodpecker lasted for a year, finishing at Christmas 1947 with a total of 280,000 tons of timber shipped.

'When I went into the first battalion, in Germany, I had never been in a battalion, I had only been in training, but in the first battalion, orders were done by bugle. I was walking one day and could hear this funny bugle call and I asked someone 'what's that' that's the fire picquet; I was the fire picquet sergeant. I ran to where we had the fire picquet as the CO and the RSM were waiting for me. But they still didn't teach me the bugle calls.

'I was then posted to VISTRE, Visual Inter Services Training & Research Establishment at Netheravon Airfield, in the MT and I was Brigadier Tullock's driver. It was rubber tanks, rubber guns, we had hundreds of them I would take the platoon out and we got the tanks and blew them up. We then had an Auster on the aerodrome, and we would go up and see what it looked like, it all looked beautiful; until the barrels started bending in the wind, it could be difficult to get the guidelines right.

'Unfortunately, the SIB [Special Investigation Branch] came down as some bright bugger had taken a photograph, I mean we all took photographs, but he sent this to Guinness. It was a bloke with a blow-up tank on his head saying, Guinness is good for you. So, the SIB came down and searched our lockers and we had to start behaving ourselves.

'After Netheravon I went to Warminster, and they did not know what they were going to do with me, so they said you are going to go to A Mess. This is the mess for majors and above, you are going to oversee that mess, I said I don't know anything about that. So, they sent me on a course to Aldershot, a catering course, I remember spending days and days learning how to take the cork out of a bottle of wine.

'So I went to A Mess, soon there was a dinner, the band was playing, and the band man said when I play 'Roast Beef of Old England' you can say dinner is served. So, I did everything, said dinner is served and they all came in. Brigadiers, Generals the lot and I realised then I had not got the wines ready and sorted. So, I went into the kitchen and there was an old sweat, he said 'What's up stripy' I replied 'I forgot the bloody wines' they were in the case but not ready. I put them all out, he said all you got to do is put the white ones in the freezer and put the red in this dixie, full of potatoes, he said that will warm them up.

'I looked and there were labels from the bottles flowing to the top of the dixie and I thought this can't be right. So, I got the red wines, I remember the brigadier wanted red wine, I went in and said, your wine sir. Very good sergeant, very good, he said. I started taking out the cork as I had been taught, twisting the bottle, not the corkscrew. Then suddenly ... BANG .... the cork and corkscrew flew straight across the mess, two chicos at the other end of the room dived under the table and the wine came out like a Molotov Cocktail. I didn't last very long in that job.

'Next, they had a cocktail party with all the dignitaries on the [officers mess] lawns. I went down the lines and told the RSM I needed some waiters. I will get you waiters he said, he gave them a 48-hour pass and a warrant. I decked them all out, the lads looked perfect. They started going around with the carafes. But what I didn't know, was they were having a drink themselves, then the brigadier came over and shouted. 'Hoddy get these buggers out; they are bloody drunk'. So, I marched them all down to the guard room, as I did, they started singing 'hi-ho - hi-ho' - I locked them all up.

'I also did a job for Combined Ops, I had two platoons and I was teaching them how to waterproof half-tracks for going on the LCT, the LCT was a nice ship. I went on board and the bosun came to me and said, your lads have been on here for 48 hours, I said yes. Do you realise that you are entailed to neaters, I said, what's neaters? He said it's the rum. In my wisdom, I said it would be better tomorrow, because at three o'clock when we are doing a dawn landing and it's to be a quiet and silent landing.

'So, I gave them all a good tot. Then as they went down the scramble net three fell off the net, it wasn't very silent after that. That did me no good either.

Ken enlisted on 25th September 1944, then re-enlisted in 1946 for five years of colour service and seven years with the reserve, I asked him if he could remember the end of his service and the return to civvy street.

'What happened is I came home, we [Ken was now married] were living with the mother-in-law, I went on a course, for agricultural engineers the reason was a bloke who did that here in Retford. I could have a month off doing that and they paid me for servicing cars, and I also got paid by the army.

'Then I realised I had to do something, you know, so I came out and got demobbed, it was 1952.

'First, I needed to get a house and I went to the housing officer, he said you will have to wait on the waiting list, but I have just come out of the army. Did you play rugby he asked? Yes, I played in the army. Well, we have just formed a rugby team in Retford, would you like to play for us. I said yes. It helped me get a house.

'I am now the president of the club, seventy years later. I played for about twenty years, I was a hooker, then I was in the singing team and today we are developing a new clubhouse.

'So, I decided to join the fire service, but I couldn't spell chimney, so I joined the ambulance service instead. I passed my driving test and I arrived at work; absolutely green I knew absolutely nothing. This bloke said to me 'now than sorry' I thought they can't even speak our language. 'Now than sorry' he said 'have you ever driven a Daimler pre-selected. Ahh, I said a Dingo. So, I got in this Daimler and went down Grove Street.

'We knocked at the door; I had the sense to pick a blanket up and I heard this voice, I am up here. We went upstairs, they were stone steps I can always remember, I followed him wondering what to do. He went up to the bedroom and he said, 'Now then what's up duck?' She said I have a pain here, he said 'You have acute appendicitis. I stood there and thought, have I come out here with a surgeon, I didn't know we had a surgeon out. Little did I know the doctor had rung and told him she had acute appendicitis; I was so green.

'He said to me 'Pick her up' so I put the blanket around her and held her in my arms, she had her head on my shoulder and she smelt a million dollars she did. I was coming downstairs, and I sensed I was going to like this job as I put her in the back of the ambulance.

'Remembering I had only been in Retford for two or three days, we were back at the station, and I was told to pick this woman up from Retford Hospital, I got in the ambulance, but I did not know where the bloody hospital was, I had to stop the ambulance, in the street and ask a bloke where the hospital was. That was my first day in the ambulance service.

'I realised then that being in the ambulance service was not like being in the army, it was all foreign to me. I had to go to St John's to learn how to stop bleeding and that, when I realised if you put a compressed dressing on a wound, you disturb the clot and if you disturb the clot, it bleeds more and that's wrong. Then I thought, fractures, it's all right in the book, with arms straight but people have fractures with bent arms and at awkward angles.

'I was going to an accident, it felt all wrong, your adrenaline was going, and you get to the scene and say lay perfectly still you are in good hands, but all you wanted to do when you got there was get them in the ambulance and get rid of them, as fast as you can.

'So, I studied and studied, I started with first aid at work. After being an instructor in the army, I took my instructor's courses. Then I took a degree from America, a Fellowship Degree, with the Institute of Certified Ambulance Personnel.

'I became the most highly qualified ambulance man in the county. So, they made me the Training Officer for Nottinghamshire Country Ambulance Service, it took me about six years.

The new-found skills and abilities Ken had learnt in the Ambulance Service were put to beneficial use when he invented a new bandage, it was known as the Hoddy Quick Clip.

It was an elasticated bandage, so it did not disturb the clot, plus it had a clip-on, so you did not have to tie a knot.

About this time Ken was also awarded The Order of St John for his work within the Ambulance Service.

Ken's in his Ambulance Service uniform

'I remember running a competition at Harrogate, I went on the stage there were hundreds in the hall, I was going to announce the winner when, up in the balcony, I saw a woman waving and beckoning to me.

'I realised it was my dad's [new] wife, so I jumped off the stage and my mates were doing mouth-to-mouth on him, we got in an ambulance with him, and they said to switch the oxygen on; I did not know how to switch the oxygen on - that is how shock affects you.

'I went to Harrogate General Hospital and the surgeon came out and said, you must have some wonderful friends, I certified your father [as dead] twenty minutes ago and they are still working on him.

'So that was the end of my father, he was aged sixty-four.

'After the war my father and mother divorced, he went to work at Lower Holme Mills in Shipley, as a foreman in the despatch department and he lived in one of the mill houses.

'I visited him after he had seen his doctor with a chest problem. The doctor said he did not have long, so gave him a year's worth of sick notes, which should have taken him to retirement at sixty-five. But he did not make it.

'I was head hunted in 1971 to go to the northeast there were over thirty applicants and I got it, I was the Regional Training Officer for the northeast, from Berwick-upon-Tweed to Scotch Corner, training all the staff and I stayed there for thirteen years.

'I absolutely enjoyed it. First, I started the early paramedics, I went around and got all the blokes who got distinction and all the rest of it, I got the budget and everything for these paramedics, saying this is what we wanted.

'I had learnt that speed is not necessary for saving lives it's stabilisation. I wanted to change it, so these paramedics, I got them through the operating theatres and everything like that.

'But I had twenty-five per cent failure rate because they could not understand blood, gasses and things like that, the technical side like heart monitors. It broke my heart.

'Then I realised where I had gone wrong, it was not them, the interview procedure was wrong, I had to have the interview procedure with A Levels rather than just caring skills. We needed more academic candidates.

'Another training plan was across the 300 ambulance stations, every city and every area had an ambulance station, and every ambulance station had an ambulance officer, and their training was all different.

'What we did was to try to get some standardisation of training, because you couldn't organise training without some standardisation. We had a chance to change with everyone in the ambulance service having six weeks of training. As you can imagine, many a bloke was saying; you can't teach me anything.

Whilst chatting with Ken he was enthusiastic about this training role in the Ambulance Service and the challenges to move forward with future developments; I ask him if his time in the army helped him at this time.

'Oh absolutely, it needed someone from the army to grab a hold of the training, you could not do anything because 'we have always done it this way' but we finally sorted it out. I am now quite proud of them.

'Another thing was a major disaster; you must actually declare a major disaster. I remember putting up a Major Disaster [a practice training exercise] with about seven vehicles and I had the ambulances going towards this disaster and this bloke came on the radio. I was waiting for him to give the call - 'This is a Major Disaster'.

'He stuttered and hesitated saying, 'err ambulances coming there there - it's a a a – it's a fucking big accident'.

'But we had more change coming, with someone saying I am going to knock that station down, that station and that station. I said you can't do that; at this time, I was a deputy.

'They never turned a wheel last night, he said, you must use your resources.

'So, we had a bit of an upset about that, he wanted to knock five stations down, and that upset me. Then there was going to be a full reorganisation, so I opted out on voluntary redundancy with full pension rights.

'In 1984 I went for an interview for a training officer at Doncaster College. I was asked to train all the college; hairdressers, plumbers, builders, everyone in all the departments had got to be trained in first aid. That soon became a full-time job, which was not the plan.

'I was there for about six years. I was also training the miners, the deputies, a lot of them had the miner's white finger and they could not tie a knot in a bandage, plus half of them had a finger off, I remember one saying that's a Friday's finger. It was after the college I finally retired aged sixty-eight.

'My first wife was, Dilys, normally known as Dal. She came from Retford; we met on VE Day dancing that night in the Market Square.

'We had one son, Stuart, who became an engineer, and he was also in a band, The Debonaires, I was even the roadie for a short while when they played with The Small Faces.

'But Dilys got dementia, I managed to hide it for two years, if I hadn't got the skills, I had I would not have been able to do it, but she died.

'We were together for sixty-four years.

In addition to the one son, Ken and Dilys, also have two grandchildren and seven great-grandchildren.

> 'After losing her I was looking at moving and living in Trinity Hospital, the Alms Houses in Retford. I was by myself for two years, which was a bloody lonely time.

> 'I could see me going into a home, which I would have hated, it would have killed me.

In retirement, Ken was still busy and determined that the War Memorial, in Retford, should be maintained, but he faced a few obstacles along the way.

> 'In the Market Place in Retford is the war memorial, it needed doing up, it was in a hell of a state. It was built by voluntary donations [after World War One] we asked the council if they could help to renovate, but they said they could not.

> 'So, I organised fundraising and got £20,000 and we did it up. I have been a custodian of the War Memorial for thirty years and have finished this last year.

> 'Looking at the names I knew some of the lad's names, but there are 360 names on the memorial from the First World War and from the Second World War there are 110. But the only information you can get about them is from the local press and websites.

> 'One story, there is Marsh and Caywood, two local lads who were at school together, two good mates, they left school at fourteen and went to Nottingham and joined the Sherwood Foresters, one of their fathers found out about it and fetched them back. The following week they went off and joined the [Sherwood] Rangers and again, he went and fetched them back.

> 'The next time they went and joined a Scottish Regiment, knowing they could not be found and fetched home. They were both killed together in World War One.

> 'So, I started working on the book, it took me about five years to produce.

Ken's book 'The Retford War Memorial – Heroes of World War One' was published in 2014 and written with Tim Bethell, a good friend of Ken and a fellow rugby player, Tim had been a teacher with an interest in local history. The book lists most of the names on the War Memorial, giving as much detail about each soldier as could be found.

Still living on his own Ken was feeling the pressures after losing Dilys, but a sudden change of events and circumstances was about to transform his life.

'I got a message saying someone was looking for me on the internet called Cornelius. I contacted them, I found it was a lady I met soon after the war when working in the mess at Warminster. She now lived in France and had five sons.

'When she was back in England, I went down to meet her. Her husband had died, she was on her own and she was thinking of coming back to the UK. After two years, we got married, I was in my nineties. My wife's name is Joan, and she is now ninety years old.

After sitting with Ken and chatting about his amazing life, I had to ask what his secret was to a long, but busy and active life.

'It is to be interested in things, all things, and be active with them, like my interest in rugby. I have come to the conclusion that no experience is ever wasted, be that a good experience or a bad experience.

'You don't think about the bad times, you only think about and remember the good times.

'But I am retiring this year from the rugby club, I have been involved for seventy years. Now if I walk halfway up the pitch, I am knackered and I feel I am letting them down by not being active enough.

Speaking to Ken, just a few days after our meeting, he had resigned as president of the East Retford Rugby Club, over seventy years after his first involvement as the club was being formed.

Donald Rose
Queen's Royal Regiment (West Surrey)

At one hundred-and-seven-years-old Donald is the oldest World War Two veteran I met while conducting my research for this book.

Donald was born at Westcott in Surrey on Christmas Eve 1914. To put that into perspective; it was the first Christmas of World War One and on that day, the well-document Christmas Truce took place, as British and German soldiers came out of their opposing trenches for a game of football in No Man's Land.

When I asked Donald his full name, he swiftly replied.

'Donald Kitchener Rose; Kitchener after Lord Kitchener in the First World War, he is the man who said [take] the King's Shilling but was killed when his boat was torpedoed; and Donald is a Scottish name because my great grandfather was Scottish, he came from Edinburgh, his name was Donald and his parents came from Islay, he married Sarah Campbell.

'My other grandfather, my mother's father, was a shepherd at Shere, not far from Westcott, he won a big cup for sheep shearing.

Today Donald lives in a residential care home in Derbyshire, where he has been for the past year. But despite living in a care home, he is still very independent and active. I sat chatting with him accompanied by his son David and Natalie who looks after Donald in the care home.

Donald is the youngest child of Thomas and Lydia Ellen Rose; Donald said his father worked as a saw-man in a sawmill in Dorking on Station Road.

'My mum was ninety-one when she died and my dad was not quite ninety, had he lived another couple of weeks he would have been ninety.

I asked Donald if his father had served in the army.

'He joined the army in 1914, he was an engineer I think he was somewhere in Wales, but I don't know what he did, but he came back after the war. He did not get his job back after the war so started jobbing gardening. Which was very poor pay, then in the winter there was no work, so no money.

Donald had two brothers and two sisters, Mabel, Arthur, Dolly and William still living at home, when he was born. Whilst Mercy had gone into service at Caterham and Tom, the eldest who was twenty-two years older than Donald, had left home to become a Catholic Priest.

'My brother Tom lived till he was eighty-five and my brother Arthur and sister Mabel were both ninety when they died. My sister Mabel had a son who joined the Metropolitan Police, he had done his two years of National Service with the RAF.

Donald went to school at the St. Joseph's Roman Catholic School in Dorking where he was taught by nuns, I asked Donald if he enjoyed school.

'I didn't enjoy anything at school, I was made to stand by the fire and got whacked for things I couldn't do. I hated school.

'The problem with my family is my mum and my dad were not Catholic to start with and my dad changed his religion, we were all expected to be Catholics after that.

'They called me a heathen because I did not believe in them.

'The only thing I could do at school was to fight because when the other kids started calling me a heathen it did not go down very well. To start with I got the worst of it, but in the end, I was the top man.

'But when I left school, I could not read or write.

When he was ten years old, Donald was paid two shillings and sixpence [twelve and a half pence] to sit and have his portrait painted by Mrs Hooper, who lived in a local country house known as The Rookery. She was a relative of the Brooke family, famous for the Brooke Bond Tea business. Donald's family are certain it was his bright red hair that was the attraction for the painting, which hung in The Rookery after it was finished.

Donald's brother Arthur was nineteen years older than him and served in the First World War with the 2nd Battalion of the Queen's Regiment, where he reached the rank of Sergeant and saw action in the Middle East, he later married Florrie Parsons and had two sons.

'My other brother Bill was torpedoed somewhere near Freetown, he was on a boat which was full of ammunition going to New Zealand, I think. When it was torpedoed, the whole boat blew up, he left two children.

Donald's brother Bill was four years older than him and married Florence Annie Johnson. Bill was too young to serve in The Great War but did serve in World War Two when he was called up into the Artillery. He was serving with the 7/4 Maritime Regiment, known as Maritime Royal Artillery, but on 11th July 1942, he was killed when his boat was torpedoed. Bill has no known grave but is remembered on the Plymouth Naval Memorial.

'On leaving school the first job I had was as an errand boy at a store in Dorking, I got the sack from there the day I started. I was talking to a young girl, but in them days you were not allowed to talk to the opposite sex. I am not sure what I got the sack for, but I walked up to Falkland Road in Dorking, with this girl. She said my dad will kill me he's just come off night work, I said no he won't. So, I said to this chap, he was out in the garden, if you beat her up you will have me to deal with, I was only fourteen and he laughed at me. I met him again about a couple of years later.

'After the shop, I went to do some building work, I learnt how to plaster, but it wasn't plaster it was cement and sand. I worked in building until I joined the army. I was working at Farnborough airport when World War Two broke out, but soon the job came to an end there and I joined the army.

Soon after joining up on his Recruits Course in Guildford
Donald is on the back row, second from the right

Donald enlisted on 26th July 1940, he was aged twenty-five, he went to the recruiting office at Guildford and enlisted into the Queen's Royal Regiment (West Surrey). In its day, the regiment was amongst the most senior English line-infantry regiments of the Army, with only the Royal Scots being senior.

'I never had to join up, but I did. There was a war on, and they needed men to fight, that's why I joined, I wanted to save this country from the Fascists. That's the reason I joined the army.

'When I joined the army, this sergeant said to me I will show you some fighting, I am going to show you an uppercut, so, I hit him. Then this Captain came shouting, 'Stop, Stop. You have killed him, look at him lying there.' He had his arms out and this other sergeant said. 'No, I don't think he is dead.' I was a very hard hitter.

'I went to join The Queens in Guildford, I did my basic training at Guildford in Stoughton Barracks, I was there for about six weeks. I remember a route march and at the end of it, a Sergeant Major said to me you will make a good corporal one day, I said I don't want to be a corporal, I was very happy being one of the boys.

I asked Donald about his time during the North Africa campaign and the D Day Landings, but like so many of his generation he did not wish to say too much, but several times said it was hard and the sights were terrible, in respect I let Donald tell his own story. Later David explained it was not unusual for Donald to get upset when talking about his wartime service, plus growing up there would never be a war film on the television if Donald was at home.

> '*I wasn't in the tank corps, but because I was in the seventh armoured division, I was loaned to them. Then when we got to Tobruk, with an officer - I was the machine gunner, we went to help the Greeks; was I pleased to get rid of them, I could not speak Greek. I was with them for about a couple of months.*'

Donald could remember a briefing, or as he called it, a lecture, from General Montgomery.

> '*He said - You are not here to run after women – that was a joke, there wasn't any – he said you are here to fight and you will fight if you get your guts blown out and head blown off, you will fight. So, I shouted out if I get my head blown off and my guts blown out can I have seven days of sick leave.*'

Following my meeting with Donald, his son David gave me a list of locations across North Africa where Donald fought, which included El Alamein, Tobruk, Mersa Matruh, and Tunis.

> '*After North Africa, I went to a place called Homs I think that is in Syria after that I was involved in the invasion of Italy.*'

While Donald was not sure it is most likely he returned to North Africa before the invasion of Italy.

> '*I remember shivering in the cold in Italy. I was like a block of ice. When I was in North Africa there was no rain, we would get lighting storms, but no rain. Italy was so cold.*'

> '*I remember after arriving an officer told me I was exceeding the speed limit you were doing forty-five, slow down. I said, 'Excuse me sir, but if the motor in front of me is doing ninety miles, I do ninety miles as you are not allowed to break convoy.' He said, 'Don't tell me a load of rubbish.'*'

When we got to our destination, he said I am going to put this man on a charge for exceeding the speed limit. Someone said have you seen the speedometer and what it says – It is in Kilometres.

After fighting his way north through Italy, in March 1945 Donald was in Germany, he had been posted to the Wiltshire Regiment a month earlier and was one of the first to reach the concentration camp at Belsen.

'I stayed with the Queens until I got to Germany then I was posted to the Wiltshire Regiment, the fourth battalion, the war was nearly over.

'I didn't enjoy Belsen, seeing all the people just skin and bones, skeletons were walking about, it was horrendous. As the war finished, I was still at Belsen, where the concentration camp is, I was there for about a year or something, that is where I met my wife, she was in the camp, I felt sorry for her and took pity on her.

Belsen, or to give it the full name Bergen-Belsen, was liberated by the British on 15th April 1945. As the allies entered the camp, they found over 13,000 unburied bodies and around 60,000 inmates. At the time of their liberation, five hundred prisoners were dying a day.

The Belsen concentration camp was originally set up as a prisoner of war camp, then in 1943 part of it became a concentration camp. After the war, Bergen-Belsen became a synonym worldwide, for German crimes committed during the time of Nazi rule.

Among the prisoners in Belsen was a young Polish girl, Zenia Linstanski born on 4th October 1921, from Vilna in Eastern Poland, which is now in modern-day Lithuania. The Germans invaded Vilna on 24 June 1941, whilst Zenia was alone in the family home.

At that time, her parents and younger siblings were visiting her grandmother some 150 miles away to the northeast at Disna, close to the Russian border, which is now in modern-day Belarus. On hearing of the German invasion of East Poland, her family fled to Russia and survived.

Zenia, aged just nineteen, was less fortunate, she was soon captured. While we do not know Zenia's full story, we know that the Germans established two ghettos in Vilna, one for Jews able to work and one for Jews incapable of work, the ones able to work were forced to work in

Jeanette and Donald soon after meeting in 1945

factories or on construction projects, while some were sent to labour and work camps in the local area. Later, the women were sent to labour camps. But despite suffering appalling conditions, Zenia survived.

David said he learnt as a young boy growing up, that Zenia worked as forced labour in an ammunition factory, where it was not uncommon for the German guards to come along and hit her around the head with a rifle butt. But whatever her story, eventually, Zenia arrived in Belsen.

Donald met Zenia amidst the worst horror and misery you could ever imagine, but they soon decided to marry.

Donald was demobbed from the army in May 1946, whilst still serving at Belsen. As he was going through his demob, he arranged for the Army to help Zenia get to England, so they could be married.

Zenia changed her name to Jeanette but was always known as Jenny. Additionally, the authorities of the time forced a change on her surname from Linstanski to Rudin.

Donald's family still does not know why, so Zenia took the name Rudin, the origins of which are also unknown.

I.B. 23(A)

Serial No. **41705**

The Bearer ~~Jeannette~~ RUDIN

is permitted to land in the United Kingdom on condition that ~~he/she~~ ~~obtains a national document of identity and produces~~ ~~to an Immigration Officer~~ + *does not* ~~and that~~ *remain in the United Kingdom longer than* TWO MONTHS.

He/~~she has stated~~/produced evidence to shew/that the details entered at 1-7 are correct.

1. Surname .... RUDIN
2. Other Names ..... ~~Jeannette~~
3. Nationality ..... Pol. 1
4. Date of Birth 3.10.21 Place of Birth Wilno
5. Documents of Identity M.F.P. 03165.
6. National Registration Identity Card Number ....
7. Proposed Address 2 Victoria Cottages, Barley Rd Westcott, Dorking
8. Description : Height .... Colour Hair .... Eyes ——— Visible Distinguishing Marks ....
9. Arrived in U.K. by Ship/Aircraft Royal Daffodil

Signature of Bearer *Jannet Rudin*

IMMIGRATION OFFICER'S STAMP.   -9 OCT 1946

(40739D) Wt 11317/281 300 Pads 5/45 H J R & L **Gp 51**

ALLIED EXPEDITIONARY FORCE

D. P. INDEX CARD

G-03550865

1. .... (Registration number) 10-35306-1
2. (Family name)   (Other given names)
3. .... (Signature of holder)   D. P. 1

Jeanette Rudin arrived at Dover on 9th October 1946, on board the Merchant Vessel Royal Daffodil, which was a troopship operating between Calais and Dover. But she was only allowed to stay for two months, or risk being deported.

Jenny and Donald were soon to be married at St Joseph's Church, Dorking on 23rd November 1946, Jenny could now remain in England and put the horrors of her time detained by the Germans behind her.

What Jenny did not know was her family, who had escaped to Russia as the Germans invaded, moved to Israel after the war. In later years Jenny visited them on an extended holiday and stayed in touch for the rest of her life.

Following the war, there was an acute shortage of housing forcing Donald and Jenny to live with his parents in Westcott. It was a small two-bedroom cottage that was also shared with Donald's sister Mabel, her young baby and his sister Dorothy.

At this time, the cottage had no electricity or gas, and the only facility for cooking was a coal range. Donald and Jenny's only child, David, was born in 1949, in Dorking.

After he demobbed Donald worked in Dorking Brickyard, but he needed a job which gave his family somewhere to live. With this in mind, he took the job of a dust-cart driver and was given one of the newly built prefabs, which were built following the 1944 Temporary Houses Act, in nearby Ashtead.

The prefab, which had a planned life of just ten years, was demolished in 1958 and they moved to a council house in Ashtead and Donald later worked as a driver and fitter at Leatherhead Gasworks.

They bought their own home in Brockham before eventually moving to their final home together in Leatherhead where they spent the rest of their lives together.

Following an extended period in a nursing home, Jenny died in February 2001, a few months before her ninetieth birthday. Donald stayed at home living alone for a short while then moved to live with David, who was now married to Sue and living in the East Midlands.

Donald stayed with them for over twenty years. But eventually, Donald's health and failing eyesight required him to move into a residential care home at the age of 106, where he has been living since.

Today, Donald admits life can be a struggle, with his eyesight as he can't see the television and his hearing has also declined, but he does enjoy living in the home.

'The dinners are good here you can't grumble about them; and the staff, you could not get a better lot of people to look after you,

'They are brilliant. They are all good friends to me.

Speaking with Natalie, she commented that Donald is still active and always ready for a chat, plus it is a regular thing for him to help other residents, passing them a tissue and opening doors.

They still see the caring attitude he had at the end of World War Two when he met his wife, about which David commented. 'He has been like that all his life as was his mother before him.

Given Donald's age and the busy life he had, I asked him what his secret was.

'I don't know why I have lived so long; I can't tell you that.

Pete Cook
Royal Navy

I met Pete at home in Bedfordshire and within a few minutes, it became clear at heart that he was still a farmer and country boy, a lifestyle he was born into and one he still enjoys. Pete now lives alone but was thankful for the support of his family, especially his daughter Anne, who joined us as we sat listening to Pete telling his story.

'My name is Peter Henry Cook, but always known as Pete, I was born on 30th October 1925 in that farmhouse there about one hundred yards away [pointing out of the window] and I have lived in the same village all my life. My parents were farmers; my mother's name was Lucy Frances Hands, and my father was Henry John Cook, my mother originated from Henley-in-Arden, Warwickshire.

'My father served in the Bedfordshire Yeomanry during World War One, he joined soon after the outbreak of war and he was commissioned in the field at Ypres. Someone told me about this recently and had some notes about it, but he certainly came home as a lieutenant after the war. He volunteered and severed during the war and then came back to farming, he was a typical and ideal cavalryman, as we had a lot of horses on the farm.

'When he came home, he did not mention much about the war, occasionally he mentioned the odd thing but not a great deal. But I remember there were several people he stayed connected with after the war, I think it was the soldiers serving under him.

The Bedfordshire Yeomanry was raised in 1794 when many counties formed a force of Volunteer Yeoman Cavalry, which could be called on by the King to defend the country, during the Napoleonic threat. The Bedfordshire Yeomanry Cavalry was disbanded after the Napoleonic Wars, but in 1901 it was re-constituted as the Bedfordshire Imperial Yeomanry for the Boer War. Then as part of a newly formed Territorial Force became the Bedfordshire Yeomanry in 1908, before serving in The First World war where they would receive several battle honours.

> 'My father had a younger brother, my uncle Bert, who did not join up. Also, a brother whom I think was slightly older, who was badly gassed in the Great War, my uncle Percy. He was discharged and to be honest, led a depressing life because of it, he lived alone the for rest of his life, the war made a mess of him.

> 'We are originally a Devonshire family coming from Chagford on Dartmoor, my grandfather came here and bought several small farms, then when he died my father bought this farm we are living in now. My grandmother was very traditional, she always wore black including a black hat, whilst my grandfather was a noticeably short man. This is surprising as my father was over six feet tall, a big man.

> 'I had a sister Joan, who was five years older than me, she married an army captain who served in Italy during World War Two, whilst Joan served as a civilian at Bletchley, not the decoding place, but I know it was a busy job. Then I have a younger brother who did not serve in the war.

> 'I went to the local village school until I was about ten or eleven, then went to Bedford school, I did not learn a lot, I was a hammer and chisel man. I was never good a maths and the like, but I got on and made a living after leaving.

I asked Pete if there was anything he especially enjoyed at school; without hesitation, he said. 'Going home, I wasn't a school lad, I was a country boy.'

> 'My father did pay for me to go to the Bedford school after I had passed the entrance exam. I went initially on the bus, then my father said he was not paying the bus fare, I will buy you a bike. So, I had to cycle every day, irrespective of the weather, seven miles each way.

> 'The only sport I enjoyed was shooting, I started with an airgun as a young

lad then I had a .22 rifle, also a .410 [shotgun] after that I owned a wide collection of guns and still enjoy shooting.

'I left school at fifteen and came to work on the farm, it was about the time of the outbreak of World War Two. We were still milking, and it was by hand, it was later we went to machine milking. We were a mixed farm with arable plus cattle and sheep, plus we reared all our own horses. I did enjoy it, but then I did not know anything else.

Living on a farm and enjoying the rural village lifestyle it is not surprising that as Pete was growing up, he had a regular assortment of animals that he reared, including some goslings.

'I still remember that small gaggle of goslings, I had left school, but it was before I joined the navy. I remember one day looking and counting them, I was sure some were missing, plus one looked a bit rough, with all its feathers looking dishevelled. The next day I went out to check on the goslings to see this cat sitting and watching them, it was eyeing them up. That explains it I thought, I shot at this cat, and it dropped into the water trough.

Unbeknown to Pete the cat was owned by a young lady that lived down the road, to use Pete's own words she played merry hell with him, then tore him to shreds and well and truly put him in his place. The young lady down the road was called Joan, she was aged just fifteen. Pete or Joan did not know as she ripped into him that morning that they were destined to be married.

'I volunteered for the navy; in fact, I ran away. Then the Red Caps [military police] sent me back. What happened was most of my friends had been called up, we were only a small group, but they were all joining up, and I thought why should I be stuck at home?

'I ran away from home to the Dover and St James Halls in Northampton; this great big man looked at me and said. 'What do you want sonny.' He did not half make me feel little. Soon I was escorted onto the next bus home. I do not know if it was my mother or my father that tipped them off, but they noticed I was not around, they knew. I had not mentioned to them wanting to join up, but they knew.

'I was exempt from a military call-up due to working on the farm. But in

Back working on the farm soon after leaving the Royal Navy

our village, all the lads were being conscripted, so I had to do my part.

'I went back the next day and the same fellow said, so you are back then sonny and asked me what I wanted to join, The Royal Navy or the Royal Marines; I remember saying I do not know – but I want to go to sea. He said Navy then. At that time, I did not know the difference between the Royal Navy and the Royal Marines. I was only seventeen, so had to wait until I was eighteen. Then in October, I got my call-up notice. I can remember the envelope arriving, a big brown envelope, I was so nervous I did not want my breakfast.

'I had to go to HMS Collingwood, near Portsmouth, I had never been on a train on my own, it was the day they bombed Luton, I remember catching the train at the local station.

I asked Pete if his parents went down to the station to see him off.

'You must be joking, if you want to join up then off you go was my father's response. I was not pampered. I walked to the station, then a train to London then down to Portsmouth.

Pete left home just before his eighteenth birthday as he headed for the Royal Navy, saying goodbye to the life he knew on the farm.

'The first thing was a haircut, then they sent me to the dentist. I know my teeth were not perfect, but I said if you are going to take one out take the lot out. He did, without delay, then and there, which was my first big mistake. I did not get on very well with the food that really was an education, plus it was the first time I had been away from home by myself.

'I soon made a lot of good friends but regard myself as one of the lucky ones. About the third night they [the Germans] bombs us, we were in the air raid shelters but the shelter just two away was hit badly, with many casualties. We were in and out of the shelters all the time as Portsmouth was bombed.

'I was there for about twelve weeks of training then I got my first draft, to Whale Island at the gunnery school. That is where I learnt you did not loiter or would find yourself running around with your rifle over your head.

'After my gunnery course, I went to Inveraray in Scotland, it was March 1944 and I was drafted to HMS Quebec, a commando training base and part of Combined Operations.

'I had only been there a few days when my chief came over, he was a nice bloke. He said they were putting me on to the LCP(L)s [Landing Craft Personnel (Large)]. I did not have a clue what he was talking about, but I soon learned. About twenty of us did the training on the LCP(L)s which were a nice craft, I was there for several months.

'Then the chief came to me one day and said there is a draft coming in for you Cook, he said I was going to a mine lifter. That only lasted for about three days when it was hit by an LCT [Landing Craft Tank] and she had a wooden hulk, so I was back again at HMS Quebec. On my return, I went to the Captain's Launch as the bowman, which did regular runs across the loch from Inveraray.

'I can also remember picking up the laundry wagon which went to Dunoon, just for a change of scenery, as it could be quiet. I also remember going out one day and meeting a local hill farmer, after some time he would ask us in and his wife would make us cakes, I remember he lived on the way down to Lochgilphead. I enjoyed my time, the countryside was like chalk and cheese from Bedfordshire, but I had an enjoyable time, I was there for several months.

'I remember one day when I was told I had a job to do and needed to smarten myself up, the Captain of HMS Quebec came down with this little, short fellow, he had a trilby hat on and a long coat. As he was getting off, he shook my hand then turned around and said, good luck men. Later I found it was King Haakon of Norway; it was just two days before D Day.

'I then remember some of our boys coming back to HMS Quebec, after D Day to recuperate. They were not wounded it was shell-shock, just young lads like us.

'I stayed at HMS Quebec until just before Christmas 1944 when my draft came for HMS Quoich, she was brand new and had not even done sea trials.

HMS Loch Quoich was one of the Loch Class anti-submarine frigates built for both the Royal Navy and several allies during the Second World War. The Quoich was named after an inland loch near The Isle of Skye, the name coming from the traditional two-handled Scottish drinking bowl, other ships were named after Loch Lomond and Loch Fyne. The Quoich was ordered in January 1943 and built at Blyth, she was launched on 2nd September 1944 ready for sea trials which were finished in January 1945.

'I was part of the skeleton crew [for the sea trials] on HMS Loch Quoich and joined her at Tobermory, on the Isle of Mull. She had been towed up from Blyth ready for trials. When I joined, I had never been on a ship before.

'I remember the trails, it was bloody rough, then the old man said weigh-anchor; one of the stokers came up he was six foot plus, he hit this anchor and away it went. It all went, the cable and the lot, the dockers had not fixed the cable. So, we lost the anchor on the sea trials, I nearly laughed, but at the time I dared not.

'With the sea trials over, we were ready for sea and went to Londonderry. Then in February 1945, we were to be part of the 24th Escort Group and picked up the first convoy from Londonderry to Gibraltar, I was really green and had never seen a convoy before.

'You learnt fast and soon got comfortable with the daily routine, we all had a hammock, and we all had a watch to keep and if you were late, you were in trouble. I adapted quite early and when I did, I enjoyed it.

'I can remember a large map with lots of crosses on it, being nosey I asked what the crosses were. Known submarines came the swift reply. We had only been out for half an hour when the sirens went, as we had our first ping from one of the submarines. That is what it was like day and night.

'On VE Day, [8th May 1945] there was a message from Admiral Donitz [the German admiral and Supreme Commander of the German Navy] to say that all U-Boats operating in the Irish Sea and the Atlantic were to surface with muzzle covers on. The ship's company on HMS Loch Quoich were privileged to board three of them. I boarded just one, they were only young lads like us. There was an officer, a chief and four or six ratings, I would say they were glad to see us, as we knocked the hell out of some of them.

'When we boarded there was a language problem, but we had no problems with them at all, I can remember waving to them as we took them in. We were in the Irish Sea and escorted them into the Foyle estuary [River Foyle into Londonderry] they were then tied up from stem to stern on both sides of the river.

HMS Loch Quoich was also involved in Operation Deadlight, the Royal Navy operation to scuttle the captured or surrendered German U-Boats, following VE Day and the end of the war in Europe.

'Also on VE day, the old man shouted to splice the main brace and we did, heavily. We did not splice it again until VJ Day, by then I was in the Indian Ocean.

Following VE Day HMS Loch Quoich sailed via Port Said, Suez and Aden into the Indian Ocean and Colombo where she would carry out numerous patrols. Including several calls to Bombay then eventually, to Malaya and Singapore. In August 1945 HMS Loch Quoich was involved in Operation Zipper, a British plan to capture Port Swettenham or Port Dickson in Malaya, then use them as staging areas for the recapture of Singapore.

However, due to VJ Day and the end of the war in the Pacific, Operation Zipper was never fully executed.

HMS Loch Quoich was also involved in escorting the infantry landing ship HMS Persimmon to Sumatra, onboard were troops of the Lincolnshire Regiment who would be present at the official surrender.

Diamond Park
Bombay India

'In the far-east half of them did not know the war was over as we went around all the islands. We invited all the children on board, we made extra bread for them, they had been living on just rice, so they were sick all over the place. We found a lot of their mothers, but very few of their fathers, remembering the Japs had been occupying their islands.

'We did come across Japanese [soldiers] on some islands, in fact, we had a Japanese General on board to help, we picked him up on Benkoelen Island. [there are variations in the spelling, but this comes from Pete]. The ship had called there and put landing parties ashore, to close a gold mine and bring the gold bars back, a British Major and a Red Cross nurse had been murdered on the island, but I believe the Gurkhas sorted that out.

'The Japanese General was the go-between and spoke good English. The one thing we were not happy with was he took over the navigator's cabin, as he was a senior officer and under the Geneva Convention that is what he was entitled to. He had two guards every day, which did not go down very well with the lads, plus he was not allowed on board with his ceremonial sword our skipper was commended for not allowing him onboard with it.

On 1 November 1945 HMS Loch Quoich left Padang in Sumatra with the task of sinking a Japanese merchant ship, the Senko Maru, which had been seized by Indonesian rebels the previous month and was seen as a threat to shipping and the fragile peace in the area. As Pete remembers that was the first and only time, he fired HMS Loch Quoich's four-inch guns.

'There was one island where we witnessed a subterranean volcano, it put the fear of God up me, as I could see this waterspout. The island was about four miles away, it had a wireless station on it and then this massive spout of water erupted. When we got there everything had gone nothing was left, including the island, animals and people were floating around, it was horrible.

'Another incident was an island near Java, it was only a small island, we were at anchor about a quarter of a mile out when we could see this small boat rowing out to us. On board was the island chief who was delivering us a pig, it was still alive, he was bringing it out as a thank you to the ship's crew. I do not know but I guess like so many of the islands they had suffered at the hand of the Japs. The skipper shouted asking if I could sort the pig out ready for the galley, yes, I replied. However, the medical officer thought injecting the pig was more humane and better. Anyway, before he arrived, I had sorted the pig and was already starting to butcher it. But despite my best efforts, I was damn annoyed when the offal was thrown overboard, especially as I love pig's liver. There was not much meat, it was only a small pig, so it was only served in the officer's wardroom.

'I can remember we had a new 2IC join the ship, a new Jimmy, we were chatting one day when he asked me where I came from, Bedford I said. So, being me, I said where do you come from? Henley-in-Arden. Do you know the Hawks family, I asked. Marjorie Hawks he said. Yes, she is my aunt, I replied. After that, I could do no wrong.

'His name was Malcolm Jefferson, I can remember seeing him after the war, it was October 1946, in Birmingham, he was busy but said to call and see him as he gave me his address and telephone number. So, I went, it was a

Gibraltar after Pete finished his first convoy
he is in the back row on the left

*massive house, I knocked on the door and the butler answered. Mr Cook,
he said; yes, that is right. I am so sorry sir, but Sir Malcolm has been called
to an urgent appointment and cannot meet you as planned. But said I
have something for you, it was my Crossing the Line Certificate, he had
them all printed and gave me one, it still hangs in the hall today.*

A line-crossing ceremony is a tradition when a ship crosses the Equator,
it is used to commemorate anyone in the ship's company's first-time
crossing. It is a rite of passage that has evolved over many centuries and
is still performed by service personnel at sea today. History would show
that in past times, line-crossing ceremonies have sometimes become
dangerous. Pete had his line crossing sailing from Borneo to Singapore on
25th September 1945.

*'I can remember being in Bandra, just outside Bombay, there was a
recuperation place run by a British missionary. We were there for about a
week, three of us Cutts, Cook and Baldwin we were always together. We
had a walk out one day and found some bananas in a tree in a garden, so
we had a plan; we knew the route and as I was the smallest and the most
athletic it was me to climb the tree. I climbed over the wall and all hell let
loose. I remember seeing a cutlass and a big dog for a start; the story goes
I ran the fastest and got back to the ship before anyone else.*

'I was in Bombay when Malcolm Jefferson came up to me and said. You are going home Cookie, I asked him what he meant. He explained I had an early release due to my reserved occupation, then he added you are going home next week, which I did. I was then sent to Columbo and told to make my way home, I joined the Katrine, which was in the same escort group right at the beginning of my naval service, and then came back to Portsmouth, it was June 1946.

'I was demobbed in Portsmouth, on the second or third day I was asked which school I went to, so I told them, and they said you join that group over there. Then I was told I was going to Dartmouth; I had no clue what Dartmouth was. But I was told it was a training college - not on your bloody nelly I replied.

'I left the navy and went back to the farm. In the Navy, I went from a boy to a man overnight.

I asked Pete what it was like to return to the farm and what his parent's response was to him being back.

'Still as brutal as ever, for whatever reason my father always seemed to pick on me, then after the navy he still did. He said he had a farm for me lined up in a local village, it was up for sale, a council farm with a preference for ex-servicemen. But it did not happen, so I came back to work on the farm and never left it.

'It was hard getting back to work, the manual work, we were still breeding all our horses, I would ride them and break them in, plus we were still milking. We had four Land Girls arrive every day, I am still in touch with one she is now one hundred and two, living in Norfolk.

'It was a tough time when I returned to working on the farm, money was tight, and I was not earning as much as I did in the navy. Four pounds and ten shillings [fours pounds and fifty pence] a week is all I had; my father did not take much more. The change over the next few years was massive, there would be twelve men lined up every morning before I went into the navy, then combines arrived and tractors got bigger, but you could not afford them at first, so it was a real struggle.

'But when I retired with all the modern equipment available, there were just two of us working the farm.

Returning to the village and the farm from the navy, Pete and Joan were soon married at Saint Paul's Church in Bedford, which was described by Pete as a big family wedding. After which they set up home in one of the farm cottages. Pete and Joan went on to have four daughters, then when Pete's father retired, he moved into a bungalow, while Pete and Joan moved into the farmhouse.

'Joan's father served in the war, he was recused from the beaches at Dunkirk in May 1940, then he was with the Desert Rat in North Africa, while her mother worked in a hospital for many years.

'I remember Joan also had a brother who joined the navy after the war, but after a few weeks, he asked his mother for money to buy himself out, saying he could not stand the strain. But she said no, you joined so stick it out, which he did, it was the making of him.

'After we got married Joan would call me Ped, but then I did call her Jar, it was our nicknames for each other. There was nothing that Joan could not do, she helped on the farm and did all the bookkeeping as well as her work in the doctor's surgery as a receptionist. In fact, she was known as Doctor Joan. We had a great life together, we travelled all over, often going back to the places I visited with the navy.

Sadly, Pete lost Joan, just eighteen months ago to cancer, which she was first diagnosed with almost two decades earlier, but as Pete said it was only in the last few months that she was really poorly due to it. Joan was aged ninety-three and they had been together for seventy-five years.

'We still have the farm, but the farming is done on contract by a neighbour, and he does an excellent job of it, but we finished with the dairy herd.

Today, Pete aged ninety-seven lives a very independent life, Anne his eldest daughter, will come and stay with him which helps with his many meetings and appointments, as despite his age he still lives a remarkably busy life. When asked what he puts his long and active life down to Pete had no hesitation in replying.

'Hard work, I still work even at my age, I have a big garden, but I do now have a gardener to help me, but he does not do the vegetable plot.

'I have always been told if a job is worth doing it is worth doing properly

Joan & Pete
at the village church

and never leave a job until tomorrow if you can do it today

'*I am out every day, sitting in a chair does not help you at all. I have had a couple of falls which have slowed me up – I have one of the motorised chariots now – but on Saturday, I am going clay pigeon shooting.*

'*But of all the things I have done, I love animals, I have enjoyed farming and rearing animals; you can have a right old cow that can produce a lovely calf.*

'*But all that said, my time in the Royal Navy did open my eyes.*

Ron Stevenson
Royal Air Force

Ron lives in Derbyshire with his partner and full time carer Pauline, in a bungalow on the edge of town. Ron was very keen to share his story, but as we sat and chatted, he struggled with his memory due to his advanced diagnosis of dementia, this resulted in him occasionally having a problem with recollections of his RAF service.

'My name is James Ronald Stevenson, but I have always been known as Ron. I was born in Ilkeston on 26th March 1924. My father's name was William he worked in a local hosiery mill as did mum, known as Hilda Mary, her maiden name was Marriot.

As we spoke Ron is not aware of any family members having served in the forces and cannot remember any uncles in uniform or talk of military service as he was growing up. This could make Ron the very first in his family to have joined up for military service.

Ron's father died when he was aged about seven and his mum remarried, Ron had a younger sister called Doris who on leaving school went to work at the offices of Boots, the chemist, in nearby Beeston.

Ron went to Bennerley School in Cotmanhay, he left at fourteen, then went to work in the drawing office at Beeston Boilers, whilst attending a training course to qualify as a draughtsman.

Ron stayed in the same job until he joined the RAF.

> 'I enjoyed school, especially drawing and art, which is the reason I became a draughtsman, plus I enjoyed cricket and football.

Ron joined the RAF after the outbreak of the war as a volunteer, joining at the Derby recruiting office.

Ron is sure he did his initial training at RAF Newton but sadly could not remember where he went to do his trade training. However, when he loaned me his Flying Logbook, I was able to put together a little about Ron's time in the war.

Ron before going to South Africa

Ron qualified as a Tow Target Operator in April 1943, this meant he was responsible for a massive windsock that was towed behind a plane that was then used as a target by air gunners, chasing them in another plane. When I discussed this with a friend who served for many years in the RAF, he simply commented – It was a bloody dangerous job.

From March 1943 to 2nd July 1943 Ron was serving at 7 AGS [Air Gunnery School] based at RAF Stormy Down, near Pyle, Bridgend in South Wales. Opened in 1940 at the outbreak of war, RAF Stormy Down was used by several RAF units but was primarily an armament training school, including air gunners training and a bombing and gunnery school.

Sadly, a total of nineteen accidents were recorded whilst 7 AGS were located Stormy Down.

After the RAF departed, the airfield was used by the French and then the Americans, flying stopped in August 1944 and it was officially closed in 1945.

In July 1943 Ron moved to 3 AGS at RAF Mona, which is on the island of Anglesey, North Wales, interestingly Mona is Latin for Anglesey. The airfield dated back to the First World War when in 1915 Royal Naval Air Station Anglesey was established there. In 1941 RAF Mona became home to 3 AGS, at the time they had eight Miles Martinet target tug aircraft which were replaced by the Anson in October 1943 and soon the school was re-located to RAF Castle Kennedy.

Ron also moved to RAF Castle Kennedy on 3 November 1943, situated in southwest Scotland where 3 AGS flew Blenheim, the Hampden and Wellington aircraft, in addition to the Defiant and Lysander aircraft used for towing the targets.

> 'I can remember training in Lysanders then after that, you moved to the big boys, I liked the Wellington.

This would almost certainly be when Ron was at RAF Castle Kennedy from July to December 1943.

Extracts from Ron's Flying Logbook indicate he was qualified on the Lysander on 15th April 1943 and the Martinet on 14th June 1943, as a tow target operator at RAF Stormy Down. To quality, he had a flight on 7th April in a Lysander flown by Sergeant Sims, in the next ten days he had a further three flights, all in Lysanders, with a total flying time of just under five hours.

Ron's last entry, as a tow target operator, was at RAF Castle Kennedy on 27th December 1943 when his pilot was Sergeant Mielnicki, most likely to be one of the many Polish pilots. The flight is shown to be a double sleeve lasting for one hour and thirty-five minutes. This was the final time Ron flew as a tow target operator.

Ron can remember failing a medical examination which forced him to stop flying, due to hearing problems, but he cannot remember when this was; but thinks it was soon after arriving in South Africa or just before he went there. This looks to be correct, as in March 1944 Ron was posted to GHQ RAF Pretoria.

The only other entry in his logbook was a flight in South Africa from Port Elizabeth to Pretoria, in August 1945, where it was noted, that the weather was very favourable.

Ron in South Africa now a MT Driver

One thing that Ron did remember was playing cricket against other RAF squadrons in South Africa, where he was selected as the wicket-keeper, he can also remember playing football.

When I asked if he could remember any friends from his time in South Africa.

> *'I can remember Harry Atkinson, he lived in Yorkshire, I lived in Derbyshire, we met in training and stayed friends, he went to South Africa, we worked together, then there was Bill he was Harry's brother.*

After stopping flying Ron had several roles, but most of his time was as a driver for his Wing Commander in an old Ford car.

> *'I went down a gold mine and a diamond mine with the Wing Commander, whilst in the diamond mine, I was given a diamond, which was illegal.*

Despite his memory, Ron can remember being in South Africa on VE Day. Plus, he remembers meeting incredibly good friends, then following his demob returning to South Africa for holidays.

Then a story slowly revealed that Ron was going to get engaged on his return home, the plan was to use the diamond in the engagement ring. But on board the ship, returning to England someone stole the diamond.

But he could not report the theft as he should not have had the diamond in the first place.

> 'Her name was Nancy, I asked my friend, Harold, to take a letter to Nancy when he went home on leave, which he did. But whilst on leave, he started dating her.

Ron found this out when Nancy sent him a *'Dear John'* letter saying she had left him.

Ron before leaving South Africa

The story goes that Nancy and Harold later married and spent a full and happy life together.

Before Ron was given the illegal diamond, he had bought an engagement ring for Nancy in South Africa. To add insult to the injury when the *'Dear John'* letter arrived whilst Ron was returning to England, in his temper at learning what had happened, Ron threw the engagement ring overboard and it still sits somewhere at the bottom of the Bay of Biscay.

> 'On returning to England, I was still a sergeant, I was demobbed in Yorkshire, then went home for two weeks leave and back to work at Beeston Boilers in the drawing office, there was little change in the years away.

Ron returned and settled in Ilkeston after he demobbed from the RAF. He soon met Sybil who lived opposite his parents, even though they has known each other for most of their lives.

Sybil's father, John Buck, was a coal miner at Bestwood Colliery and her mother's name was Lillian, Sybil worked in the offices at Boots, along side Ron's sister Doris.

Ron and Sybil married on 5th June 1948 at St Mary's Church in Ilkeston, in what Ron remembered was a grand wedding. Soon after getting married, they bought a house, which had just been built.

After getting married Ron and Sybil travelled widely, often with Ron's sister Doris, mostly across Europe but at times further afield, but they had no children.

In older age, Sybil was diagnosed with dementia and cared for by Ron for as long as he could, but she was forced to move to a residential care home, she was now in her late seventies.

Sadly, Sybil's dementia became worse and she passed away over twenty years ago. Ron then lived on his own, in the same house they had bought after getting married.

Pauline, Ron's current partner, has been a friend of the family, as had her late husband, for over thirty years. During that time Pauline and her husband helped Ron following the loss of Sybil.

It took until the recent pandemic before they moved in together, both now widowed and living alone, plus Ron's dementia was getting worse.

I enjoyed my time sitting with Ron, despite the struggle with his memory due to his advancing dementia, I learn much about a quiet-natured and well-mannered man who served in South Africa during World War Two, plus he was the first tow target operator I had ever met.

Jack Dickinson
25th Dragoons

Jack lives on his own, supported by his family and neighbours in Worksop. Within a few minutes of sitting and talking it became clear that Jack wanted to chat about his life, not only in the RAF and army, as he has served in both but also about his family.

'I was christened John Dickinson, but have always been known as Jack, as were both of my grandfathers. I was born on 17th October 1925 in Rhodesia, not the African one, the one near Worksop in North Nottinghamshire, but I left there when I was five to live at Langold because my dad worked at Firbeck, which was a new pit then. He was a Geordie and came down with his family from Newcastle, they were all coal miners Then he met my mum in the Worksop area.

'My dad's name was Robert Wilson Dickinson; I don't know where the Wilson was from, I can't remember any relations called Wilson. My mum's name was Doris May Duckmanton Johnson, she came from Whitwell. Her family had lived there for many years, some of them worked down the pit, but my grandfather was a butcher in the village.

'My mum's name, Duckmanton; I gather there was an aunty in Australia or New Zealand, who had a lot of money, she said anyone who used the name Duckmanton will get some money when I die. It happened, when she died my mother got a share.

'My dad served in the 1914 – 1918 war in India, I don't know much about what he did in the Great War, but I think he was with the Royal Engineers. I know he joined as the war broke out, but he was soon discharged as he caught malaria. My dad never mentioned the army much, we only spoke about India, after the war he went back to the pit.

'I had two brothers, both younger than me, Peter Wilson – Wilson after my father, he worked in the office at Firbeck Colliery. Then there was Stan who was also called Stanley Robert – again after our father, he was my youngest brother and worked in the fitter shop at the colliery, a surface job not down the pit.

'Neither Peter nor Stan ever went into the army. I often wonder why my two brothers took my father's names, but I was just Jack.

'I can remember when I was young my mother had a sister, Gladys, who lived in Rhodesia, we would go there at Christmas all the family got together, we spent every Christmas together. There were five in our family and more than five of them, when we got together, we would all squeeze into bed sleeping head to toe.

'Then when I was in the army, I got a letter from my mother to say my uncle Willis had been killed at Shireoaks pit, I don't know what happened. He was my mother's sister's husband, Gladys. I knew him very well.

Willis Stocks was aged forty-eight, living at 1 Marjory Street, Rhodesia when he was killed at Shireoaks Colliery on 3rd June 1947. The inquest was held just three days later at the Courthouse in Worksop, the details recorded as; 'Knocked into the sump, by tubs'.

'Uncle Willis was a chapel preacher at Rhodesia, plus my uncle Norman was part of the chapel, which meant when we went on holiday together, I had to go to chapel.

'Growing up was a very happy time I would go to Rhodesia for a month at a time, we may not have gone on holiday often as we did not have a car, but I can remember going to a caravan, at the seaside, but I don't know where it was. My granddad had a car, he lived at Weston-on-Trent, and he would pick us all up for a week's holiday, that was my mother's father after he retired from the butcher's shop.

'A lot of my pals growing up went down the pit, but my dad said one down a coal mine is enough, he had one or two accidents at one time and another.

'The school was just across the road from our house, I went from Infants to juniors then seniors at Langold School and left at fourteen. I should have left at fifteen, but the war broke out [World War Two] so they knocked it back to fourteen, it was fourteen originally and that was the year they changed it, as they wanted people in the army and to get to work.

'I enjoyed school it was all right; I played a bit of football, but I did not get on with all the teachers. I remember one teacher called Mr Garner, as we lived opposite the school, we could hear him in our house when he got his temper up. I remember some years later being on a bus, I was in the army then, and he got on the bus and came over and made a real fuss of me saying I should go back to the school for a talk, I said yes, all right; but I never did.

'I was very average at school, I just kept out of trouble, as well as football which I played for the Firbeck Colliery team I also played a bit of cricket, just little local leagues.

'As I left school, I went to work in a wood yard in Worksop, Godley and Goulding on Eastgate, they had a lot of big saws; that's one thing I got off them [as Jack pointed to a thumb and finger both still showing the scars] I had only been there a couple of days. I was off work for so long, then I went back to doing the same job.

'On Eastgate is a big house and that is where the mechanic lived. I had to take all the waste wood offcuts to his wife, Mrs Godley, for the fires in the house, she was German, he met her during the war, the 1914 – 1918 war. She asked me one day if I enjoyed my work and I said there was nothing in it really; so, she asked would I like to work in a garage, and I said yes. The following Monday when I got to work, they told me I was working in the garage. It was Godley and Goulding's garage, but it was her that got me the job. I stayed there until I went into the army.

'The garage looked after all the timber yard vehicles, they taught me about engines and servicing vehicles, it was a big yard and at sixteen I could reverse the big lorries into the shed and change tyres, some of which were massive.

'At Langold we had stairs in the house, and we were told that the safest place was under the stairs, my dad told us to get under there, as he worked a lot of nights, so my mum and two brothers would get under there. I sat there many times; you could hear the planes come over bombing Sheffield. Then you got the wardens coming around shouting, get that light out, then come banging on the door, get that light out, for a little chink in the curtain.

'We had a lot of bombers flying over, they made a right mess of Sheffield, we sat under the stairs for hours and you could hear the planes go over then the bombs going off.

'I was conscripted into the forces, it was either joining up or going down the pit, but as my dad said one down the pit is enough. There were a lot of accidents down the pit in those days, my dad had scars all over him. I was eighteen and got a letter for a medical at Mansfield, in an old chapel which had been made into a medical and recruiting place. The RAF bloke said we would like you in the RAF, but you have a wonky eye and I don't think we want any more ground staff. So, I went to the army bloke, he said yes you are fine for the army, we will let you know more. I went home expecting to join the army.

'Then I got a letter saying I was in the RAF. I did my square-bashing course, then after a bit, I went to RAF Locking in Somerset to do a flight mechanics course, so I was going to be ground crew, not flying. I enjoyed the course, every Saturday night we went to Weston-Super-Mare where I met a few girls. I passed the course and then went on my first seven days of leave in my RAF uniform, feeling very proud.

'After my leave, I went back to Locking, then on the following morning's parade, I was told you are in the army as from today so get your kit together as you move out tomorrow. It was not just me; it was a load of us. We went to Liverpool to swap our kit over, then we were all posted to whichever branch of the army we were going to.

'I went to the tanks at 52 Training Regiment at Bovington, there were a lot of recruits there for driving and a lot of guardsmen on the tank courses.

'There was more square-bashing to convert us from RAF to the army, you did foot drill first then you did rifle drill. As we were passing out you needed a coin to keep the magazine down. I can remember picking my rifle up and the bloody penny jumped out, everyone had finished, and I was struggling to get the magazine down.

'One day we could not get on the square it was being resurfaced or something, at the back of the gym where all the barrels for it. As we marched past, this sergeant, he was a good sort, but was walking backwards.

'Then he went backwards, falling over one of the barrels. We all laughed, as we were marched back to our billets, I still had a bit of a grin on my face, when this corporal came over and said. 'I will put you where the birds won't shit on you.'

Jack, after being transferred to the army

'I was at Bovington for about six months, after more square bashing, we learnt tank driving and lorry driving. I was very lucky as I had a driving licence, I got one at seventeen, and we did lorry driving before going onto the tanks. About six of us were on the back of this lorry and they shouted come on let's have one of you in here; my mates pushed me forward because I could drive.

'It was Corporal Hazel, he sat there telling me what I should and should not do, I never said a word. Then he said go on then start. I pulled away, changed to second then third, but when you changed down you had to rev up every time, as there was no synchromesh in them days. He then said to me you can drive, can't you? I still said nothing.

'I made some good friends on that course, one was a mate in Brighton, I could get to Brighton with him for a weekend, but not always get home. He was Bill Gasson, we stayed in touch for years, he came to my wedding, and I went to his.

'After Bovington, it was fourteen days leave then I was on a boat to India. We docked in Bombay [now Mumbai] the ship was the SS Stratheden. I can remember going through Suez, we could go up and sleep on deck, but you were woken early and if you did not move you were wet through when they scrubbed the deck – To wake you they shouted 'Wakey, Wakey – washy decky.'

'As we arrived in Bombay, we have a free day, so we had a walk around then found a swimming pool, we hired swimming stuff and went swimming, that was my first day in India.

'We then went to a transit camp, about fifty miles from Bombay and eventually, we were posted, I went to A Squadron, but B and C Squadron plus HQ Squadron were in different places. There was no one in A Squadron when I arrived, after a bit, we were told they were still all in Burma. The place we slept in was terrible, very small and four of us had to sleep in there, it had matting sides, a thatched roof but no doors, no windows. They looked like they had been built quickly for us, but there were scorpions and snakes about.

'We also had kite hawks, that's what we were told they were, that sat in the trees. But as you walked from the cookhouse, carrying your plate of food, the kite hawks would swoop down and steal your dinner. We never would tell anyone new arriving, they had to learn. They may have been kite hawks, but we knew them as shite hawks.

'After some time, the rest of the squadron arrived and they made us up into tank crews, then this railway wagon came in, on the back all sheeted up was our tanks, but they had propellers on. After they unloaded, we got into our crews, I had a corporal tank commander. The rest [of the crew] had just come out of being in action in Burma. I don't know what happened but three or four lads from A Squadron went to investigate some Japanese, and they were never seen again. I think there is a memorial in Burma for them, no one had any idea what happened to them.

The DD Tank or Duplex Drive Tank, soon earned the nickname *Donald Duck* due to its ability as an amphibious, swimming tank. The concept was established during the Second World War, when the DD Tank was used during the D Day Landings in 1944. The DD tank was a variant of a Sherman with a flotation screen, allowing the tank to float with two propellers to drive it forward whilst floating.

Jack, on the right, at the Frontier in North West India

'As crews, we went out to sea in them, but we never practised off a boat, coming down the ramp of the landing craft at sea. The other squadrons did but not A Squadron. Soon we got our ammunition and were given American K-rations, they were bloody horrible. We started training and we continued training, taking the tanks out to sea.

'Then the training was finished; we were waiting for a boat to pick us up to deploy. The other squadrons were loaded, A Squadron, we were all parked up waiting to go, ammunition loaded and everything. Then they cancelled it just like that. It took a few days, then we learnt the Americans had dropped the bomb on Japan that morning as we were waiting to sail. The war stopped just like that; the Japs had packed it in.

'On VJ night, or a few days after when we knew, we got a big can, and we got it filled with beer. There was nowhere to go, no electricity just lamps, to sit and write a letter home, it was a rough place.

'After this, we had to unload all the ammunition and get ready as we moved again, to what I think was an American hospital. I can't remember where it was, but it was a nice place. I can remember stacked in one corner was a load of letters that had never been opened, they were from a girl in America to an American soldier.

'But I must give them there do, all the lads who came out of Burma were soon sent home very quickly, that was good to see.

'We were now really killing time and I was put on a tank commander's course; I was happy with that as it was something to do. Then a notice went up saying I was wanted in the office, so I reported to be told they were sending four tanks, from across the regiment, to practise river crossings and I had been selected. We moved back across India once the tanks were loaded, then north.

'There were just four tanks, ready to practise the river crossing but we couldn't do it as the rivers have run dry. So, a number of us were picked out to go on leave, including me, and we went up into the Himalayas, I was there for a month.

'When we got back, they had sent all the crews back, keeping just a tank commander and driver for each tank. Back to the river crossing, our tank got stuck in the middle of the river, it was a good job we had a LAD with us, from the Indian Army, with a winch to pull us out.

'After that, we loaded up to make our way back, on the way we stopped at the Taj Mahal to have a look around, the train pulled into the sidings as someone found a problem, so I went around the Taj Mahal. We were soon back in a transit camp near Bombay, then back to the regiment at Calcutta.

'They then put a notice up with your number on and when you were going home, we only had the green uniform, they had taken our Karki off us. We went to the camp at Doolally, where we changed our uniforms. I was given a pair of trousers, but I could not get them over my boots. I went down to the tailors, and they took the big map pocket off the leg and put it into the bottom of the leg. It only took him a few minutes; I could now get my boots and trousers on.

The Deolali transit camp was a transit camp founded in 1861 for the army, about one hundred miles from Bombay, its primary use was the accommodation of soldiers arriving in India and those awaiting ships to leave.

The soldier's name for the camp was *Doolally*, which soon became a slang term associated with mental illness. Troops in the camp often had a long wait for a troop ship home and many broke down from the heat of the Indian summers, as troop ships only sailed in the winter months. Some men had to wait in the camp for months, often with very little to do. Hence the phrase the *Doolally Tap* or to have gone, *Doolally*.

The Deolali Transit Camp is also the location for the comedy series *'It Ain't Half Hot Mum'* which was based during the final months of World War Two, the very time that Jack was in India. The series is based on the experiences of Jimmy Perry and David Croft, who had both served in India during the war.

'It was February 1947 when I got back to England into Liverpool, on the MV Britannic. I went home, it was the best time of my life, it was six o'clock in the morning as they opened the door, my dad and two brothers were getting ready to go to work. We had not seen each other for two years; they knew I was on my way home but didn't know when I would get there. My brothers and dad were late for work that day.

'I had two months leave, then back to a transit camp in the north of England, there were a lot of recruits in there, I was now an old soldier so they got all the fatigues, I would go back to my billet for the morning. I can remember the Sergeant Major shouting on the morning muster parade. 'Fall out the Donkey Wallopers' which was us, the cavalry.

'Next, I went to Germany, to Wuppertal. I was mainly lorry driving there, with the Hussars. I had a regular run taking the NAAFI girls back to the centre of town after they finished work. I got friendly with a few of them, and I went home with one of them, her brother did not like it as I think her father had been killed in Russia. I was in Germany for about ten months then I got demobbed.

'After that, it was back to Worksop, and I started working again at Goodley & Goulding, I was back in the garage. I was over in the factory one day, I had been back just a couple of months, and there was a girl that I was at school with, in the same class, we recognised each other and were soon dating, then we married. Her name was Mabel Jacklin, she worked in the office.

Jack and Mable married on 22nd March 1952, at the village church in Langold, and had one son, Michael. Jack continued working at Goodley & Goulding, then moved to Oates in Worksop and finally worked at

Remploy, where he ran the stores.   Jack retired, while at Remploy, in 1991.

'Mable and I went dancing a lot we had a great life with our neighbours Ron and Margaret. We were getting ready to go out one night and I could hear a car on the drive, looking out of the window I could see Ron, I thought something was wrong, as I walked to the car Margaret came out of their house.

'Ron looked like he was having a stroke, we got him out of the car and back into the house. The ambulance took him to the hospital, but he died about four days later.

'You then go forward another a couple or three months, it was June 1990 just before I retired, Mable my wife was not very well, I said I would stay at home to look after her, but she said to go to work I will be all right. I went to work but the following day she was no better, so I stayed at home.

'I can remember tidying her pillows as she said you can put them back. I went downstairs, when I went up again, she was dead.

'Margaret had lost Ron and I lost Mable, within weeks of each other. We were always good friends and with time we talked things over and moved in together.

'We had a super time, we went to America, Canada and China. We spoke about getting married, but it did not matter, but then Margaret became ill, she died in September 2018.

Jack may have his mobility problems today, but he is still very active and busy, he is thankful for the support from his family, especially his son Michael, plus several neighbours.

But after such a full and eventful life I had to ask him if he had any secrets about his old age.

'Live it as it comes and get on with it, I mean when Mable died it came as a real shock, I was not ready for that. But then I was with Margaret.

'But you have to live your life. You need to be busy.

Ernest Tryner
Seaforth Highlanders

I met Ernest at home on the Nottinghamshire and Derbyshire border, where he lives alone, it was soon clear that Ernest was still very active despite approaching his ninety-seventh birthday.

Add to this he still had a clear and accurate memory of his time during World War Two, then as we sat, he teased me saying, I am sure this will bore you.

Above all, he gave tribute to his colleagues who served with him in The Seaforth Highlanders. Several times Ernest insisted that his part in the war was insignificant compared to the battalion, which had already fought in North Africa and Normandy by the time he joined them, and he asked that this be noted within his story.

> *'My name is Ernest William Tryner, I was born on 24th September 1925, at Hucknall near Nottingham. My mother was born at a place called John O' Gaunt, near Melton Mowbray, in 1895. My grandfather Thomas, my mother's father was on the railway and my mother was the eldest of a family of eight.*

> *'Her brother was killed in World War One on 23rd October 1918 whilst serving in the 7th Battalion of The Leicestershire Regiment, which was my uncle, William John Welsh Smith, who was a Lance Sergeant. They had moved into some open fields; he wrote home to say how nice it was to get out of the trenches.*

'Like a lot, he gave his age wrong when he joined up, and I rather think he joined at seventeen and coming from John O' Gaunt he was pushed into The Leicester's, he served in the trenches most of his time. He came home in 1916, because of what they called trench fever, which I assume is exhaustion. Then whist in hospital in Surrey he was called and sent to the Easter Rising in Dublin.

'My parents married in 1919, and for their honeymoon, they went out to France and looked for his grave. The story goes that; they went to the Imperial War Graves Commission, but they had no record, but my mother had a letter from The Padre of 7th Battalion of The Leicestershire Regiment, which told her where he was buried. They found his grave and reported it back to the Imperial War Graves Commission.

'Then I took my father out in 1970, again to find Uncle Will's grave, which we did in Amerval, there are about thirty men of The Leicester's buried there, near Solesmes close to the Belgian border.

'My father volunteered and served from either late 1914 or early 1915 to 1918 in the Army Service Corps, which later became the Royal Army Service Corps. He served for almost four years in France but never in the fighting line because he was a bit of a pioneer in the internal combustion engine. He had been bought up as a colliery fitter, he was born in 1892 so was twenty-two when the war broke out.

'From about 1911, he worked looking after the managing director's French car, a Darracq and a Daimler, which had been converted to the colliery ambulance [at Bestwood Colliery]. There were not many people dealing with internal combustion engines at that time, so he was pushed into the Army Service Corps to deal with the staff cars, he even dealt with the London red buses that were taken out to France. He finished the war in the rank of Corporal.

'After World War One, when I was a small boy at school, my father became the fitting shop foreman, he was a very dedicated man not only to his work but also to his family. He was an excellent father, I can remember him dashing home from work, getting washed in the sink and getting off to Nottingham University, catching the train to Nottingham. He got qualifications to become the assistant engine wright, they called them engine wrights then, at Bestwood Colliery.

'He then became the chief engineer at Babbington Colliery at Cinderhill on the outskirts of Nottingham, then he went to be the chief engineer of Church Gresley Colliery at Swadlincote, in the south Derbyshire coalfield at about the time I joined up in 1942.

'My mum was a cook and housekeeper to the managing director of Bestwood Colliery, which is where my mother and father met when he came home on leave in 1916 and they got engaged, they married in Twyford Church, near John O' Gaunt, in 1919. I have an older sister, Mavis, who will be one hundred later this summer, we are looking forward to celebrating her 100th birthday.

'My father was a remarkable man, he worked damn hard, I can remember taking his Sunday lunch to the pit when he was doing major repairs. He would save his money and my mother was a good organiser.

'I remember he [my father] bought a little car, when we lived in Bestwood village, people thought we were rich. I was about eight, he said to me do you want a day off school; I thought he was going mad because we never had any time off school. We set off at seven, I had no idea where we were going, we caught a train from Bestwood to Nottingham, then a train to Birmingham, then a tram to the Austin works. We then picked up a 1933 Austin Seven, straight from the factory.

'I remember a man coming out in a white coat and sitting at the front with his feet under the radiator, then with a chalk-stick beautifully put the registration number on, then said you will need to get that painted over or it will wash off. We drove home, none of my mates at school had cars.

'Plus, he spoke pretty good French as he stayed on a French farm [in the war] with a family near Saint-Omer, then he was in Honfleur. We would go to Southsea on holiday, one year he took us to France for the day from Southsea, on a paddle steamer crossing to Le Havre, he always spent his money on his family.

'We were at Southsea when war was declared in 1939, I was fourteen, all the sailors were putting their guns on Southsea common, at that time I wanted to join the navy, I was fourteen and my mother said; you are not, there is a war on. Tents were going up on Southsea common as the *naval reservists were arriving. I remember my mother saying we should get back home, and my father said, we will be all right.*

'I went to the village school in Bestwood from the age of five until eleven, then the Henry Mellish Grammar School in Bulwell I stayed there for six years, but because of the war, I only spent one year in the sixth form. The idea being you had to get to college early, so I was at Loughborough College at seventeen, instead of eighteen, I studied to be a teacher, in handicraft and PE, my first choice would be handicraft.

'Every week we had to do two half-days military training as part of the [military] exception, with the training corps, we did one afternoon in Loughborough and for the other, we were bussed to Nottingham University. We had some fun infantry training, and I had a lot of training before I was called up.

'I remember the night of El Alamein, in October 1942, I had been at Loughborough for about a month, and we were part of the Leicester Home Guard on this exercise, we marched from Loughborough to Sawley Bridge. I was training to be a PE teacher, so I was very fit.

'I got through the first year, I should have been called up in September 1943, at the age of eighteen but with the exception, I got two more terms and finished my teacher training. I was then called up and arrived in Lincoln on 1st June 1944.

I asked Ernest what it felt like to arrive for training, following his call up, just a matter of days before the news of D Day and the liberation of Europe had started.

'I can remember on June 6th being on parade in the barracks at Lincoln with aircraft coming from all directions, as Lincolnshire was like a massive landing ground, and we were told the invasion had started, we all thought we would get sent there. There was great enthusiasm amongst us at the time, we were all the same age about eighteen.

Ernest's family had for a considerable time suggested he should write about his wartime service, which he had finished before I met him; I am grateful he has given me access to his notes as he recalled his war service to me.

'I have been messing about with this story for some years, making sure I had not exaggerated because there is nothing worse. It has not been published as I get the feeling that some of the blokes around me, who had been at El Alamein had seen ten times more than I had. They had been right across the desert to Tunisia, they had landed in Sicily and Normandy.

'I must say at the outset that I was lucky to avoid the fierce fighting which occurred in Normandy after the D-Day landings.

'I reported to [Sobraon Barracks] Burton Road, Lincoln for initial training. This was routine as I had lots of training in the OTC (Officer Training Corps) at Loughborough. I was sent to Redhill, Surrey to go before a War Office Selection Board for tests to decide if you were potential officer material.

'This lasted 3 - 4 days; I got the result fifteen months later - too late, more of that to follow, and my life would have been vastly different.

'After six weeks in Lincoln, on to the Queens Royal Regiment at Maidstone for further infantry training. Here I experienced the first of the V1 flying bombs, the Doodle Bugs. I saw a number directed at London and shot down.

'Apart from miles of marching through the lanes and bye-ways and crawling in the disused chalk quarries and getting orders to clean up pronto, we did do some firing of our rifles on the ranges.

'The next stage I was posted to was Advanced Infantry Training at Southwold, Suffolk. This was obviously a toughening-up course, ready for Montgomery's army, and it certainly was. We were dropped somewhere in the adjacent countryside and given a map and orders to be at a certain pick-up point. If you did not make it, you had miles of marching back to Southwold. We were billeted in the Grand Hotel, which was not so grand and demolished after the war. Apart from the rigorous training, there were other incidents I remember well.

'After perhaps three days trekking over Norfolk and Suffolk we arrived back at Southwold and were given a foot inspection, I had blisters on both feet, like many others and ordered 'light duties and to wear plimsols'. The army compassion; Saturday - In the cookhouse washing

Ernest in Berlin taken 20th January 1946

greasy dishes and Sunday; shovelling five tons of coal at a nearby Naval Hospital.

'We were once coming back to the US Air Force station at Lakenheath, as we got near you could see the B17 bombers coming back from daylight raids, engines on fire and burning aircraft on the runway.

'The full infantry training was complete, and we were ready for battle.

'How wrong that turned out to be, that was to be learned later when under fire.

'The next stop was Shorncliffe Barracks at Folkestone, not doing very much, but it was either a posting to Europe or Burma, I was selected for the former.

'I had been in the army a few months now it was late October when we were pushed on a train at six at night and dumped at a transit camp at Eastleigh, near Southampton to spend two or three days and nights cold and miserable in some wood, in two-man tents. Then to embark on a troopship which anchored for the night off Spithead with three or four others. Our destination was Ostend, which had only very recently been cleared of mines laid by the Germans, we may have even been the very first troop ship to dock there.

'In the dark, we were then trucked to Louvain, a Belgian university city and bedded down in some part of the university. The next morning, we were trucked to a former Belgian Army Barracks at Bourg Leopard and given a bunk in the stables, it was terrible, it was cold and damp; I slept fully clothed with only my boots off and my feet inside my big pack. We were kept there for a number of weeks doing very little.

'Towards the middle of December, the Huns launched what's been called the Battle of the Bulge, a complete surprise attack aimed at reaching Antwerp to cut off supplies to the British and Canadian Armies. To meet the threat the 6th Airborne Division came out from England and a number of us were picked out to join them, I can't remember the number, but it was about twelve.

'The weather was cold, and snow lay all around but the enemy by this time had been halted, the 13th Battalion Parachute Regiment had previously been involved in heavy fighting. I didn't see much of the fighting as it was mainly over, but I joined in [their] patrols trying to find where the Germans were and in what strength - the night probes were hazardous, to say the least. I only saw the odd German at long range.

'Keeping warm and dry was the worst job. Boots and socks were always wet and sleeping difficult. The panic was soon over as the skies cleared and Allied fighter-bombers appeared in large numbers to attack the retreating German columns. That phase of the war was over and the next was about to begin.

'Still attached to 13 Para we were moved to a section of the river Maas, near Roermond where things were very quiet. I was with a section of about ten or twelve in a village by the river and our role was to patrol a length of the Maas and observe enemy movements across the other side. It was all very peaceful and no firing at all.

'Each night after dark four or five of us moved along the bank and lay up opposite a German post in the open just listening. Snow was on the ground; it was bitterly cold doing 2-hour stints. German supplies came up by horse transport, which surprisingly was the norm for German infantry.

'The Germans were great at camouflage but very noisy all night. Every night their food came up by horse transport and we heard the rattle of *cans and even some individuals swinging their arms to keep warm. This was the routine for the next ten days when our sector was taken over by an American unit fresh out from the States.*

'I returned to Bourg Leopard and a few days later I was posted to the Seaforth Highlanders, straight to the Fifth Battalion, The Duke of Sutherlands Own, it was early January 1945. They were part of the Highland Division, but often teased and called the Highway Decorators.

'After a short spell in Nijmegen, the Battalion moved to the major obstacle advancing into Germany - The Rhine. For some reason, I was never involved in the Reichswald Forest and stayed at camp. We were never given much prior information for obvious reasons.

The Battle of The Reichswald, known as Operation Veritable, occurred in February and March 1945. Fighting through the Reichswald - The Imperial Forest - was hard, but the Allied advance continued and by mid-March, they had cleared the way to the next objective – Crossing the Rhine.

'Whilst there my friend from Lincoln, Ray Nicholls, we were in the same company, C Company, said the signals officer wanted to see us. Captain Latta was the signals officer and asked me, 'What were you in civvy street'. I replied, 'A student, sir'. 'Of What' he snapped the reply. 'A teacher, I am a qualified teacher, but I have not yet taught'.

'He asked Ray Nicholls the same then asked us both. 'Can you do morse?' I told him I could as I had learnt it in the sixth form with the ATC, but I could only do about ten words a minute.

'A few minutes later the signals sergeant tapped out a message, which I managed to decode and was then posted from C Company to HQ Company, as they were short of signallers. For the next five days, Ray Nicholls and I went with the signal's corporal going through the procedure on the Number 18 Radio Set, telephones plus repairing and laying telephone lines – normally a three-to-four-month course.

'The 51st Highland Division then moved into Belgium for training in assault river crossings prior to the Rhine crossing. We received training getting in and out, plus the precise position we should occupy in these flimsy canvas assault boats, which carried ten men. They were powered by an outboard

motor and manned by The Royal Engineers.

'Then back into Holland to a concentration area in preparation for the Rhine Crossing, where the 51st Highland Division was to be part of the first assault troops to cross.

'A day or so before, perhaps 21st or 22nd March, we were given a briefing by I think the brigadier of 152 Infantry Brigade, on what was expected of us and the sort of opposition we were likely to meet and the support we may get in the shape of artillery fire etc. We knew we were in for a big fight.

'23rd March arrived and early that morning an NCO plus another signaller - I cannot remember their

Ernest on the left, with Jimmy Taylor, taken in July 1945 at Altenbruch

names - and myself were sent up to the flood bank by the Rhine.

'The bank was probably fifteen to twenty feet high, we dug in at the bottom of it in the spring sunshine, and waited not knowing what lie ahead, the battalion was out in the open behind us.

'The assault was timed for 9 pm preceded by a massive artillery barrage on German positions and artillery gun sites - It was deafening.

'My Battalion was due to cross immediately after the 2nd Battalion Seaforths, but there was some hold-up that delayed our crossing until just before dawn the next day, the 24th March. Previously we were issued with blow-up life jackets, but I have often wondered if that would have kept us afloat in full winter clothing plus the rest of our equipment - Not a chance.

'We crossed under a smoke screen and under some shell and mortar fire. The lifebelts we cut off on landing on the other side, then I realised I had not blown mine up; I can remember laughing to myself – *Once on terra firma.* We moved some distance inland and then proceeded into the small industrial area which was mostly in flames. I remember, to my horror, we passed through a blazing factory having to skirt machinery that was alight.

'Our next fight was to capture a small vital area at Groin to prevent German reinforcements from reaching the village of Rees, the battalion had to attack at night - It was to be a costly night for the Battalion.

'I was not right at the front but in Battalion HQ that day and some distance, about 200 yards, from the actual fighting, I knew they were taking a pasting, which they did. You could hear all the noise and witness the casualties. It was obvious to all the mates near me that this was a very tough battle. Later they received help from Sherman DD tanks.

'The casualties were high - I think we lost 26 men dead and a number wounded, maybe as many as 120 wounded.

'That was the worst night that I can remember, I can still remember the noise and the buildings blazing and silhouettes against them, as I looked on from my hollow with my radio set.

The battle for Groin, on the German bank of The Rhine, lasted for some thirty-six hours and was one of the costliest periods in the battalion's history. While sitting with Ernest, he told me that, the action at Groin was made into a training film by Major Graham Foster, Royal Marines, stationed at the Small Arms School Corps, Warminster.

'Major Foster learned of my part in the action from his father Ralph Foster whom I knew. Plus, his mother, Sheila, was the Deputy Head of Wilsthorpe School where I taught for twenty-six years after the war.

'Major Foster, he retired as a Colonel but described Groin as 'a hands behind your back battle' that is, no tanks, no artillery and no air support, only men with the arms in their hands.

'Following Groin, a short quiet period of laying telephone lines to the various companies, but always on the alert for snipers.

'It was about this time – I can't remember the exact day - I was the radio operator for Colonel Sym, our CO. I remember following him one day when a Moaning Minnie opened up - the German six-barrel rocket mortar – I think it was one of them. The Colonel dived into a nearby tank track, which was German, I followed him. The radio set knocked my helmet off. He lifted his boot and caught me on the cheek with the heel, it started bleeding. When we got up, he said. 'Signaller, have you been hit?'

'No Sir, No Sir'. I answered I have just caught it on something, with the blood streaming down my face.

'He never did find out the full and true story.

'We had moved further forward into the bridgehead; I think it was 29th March and it was just getting light. We in [battalion] HQ had spent the night in a cellar, which I remember was warm and dry. I must endeavour to determine precisely where this was, but I think it was at a small river crossing near Dinxperlo.

'We were suddenly stirred by the appearance of the Signal Sergeant, Willie Mcloed – I think, [this may have been Sergeant McAllen of the Signals Platoon] to announce that the Boche had appeared in large numbers, but we didn't take much notice. Then suddenly, this rocket hit the top of our cellar steps, it was probably a Panzerfaust, an anti-tank rocket.

'Soon the CO, Lt Colonel Sym said. 'Look we are surrounded, we need to surrender, otherwise, they would only throw grenades down on us.'

'I sent a quick final radio message to the rest of the unit. 'We are being overrun. We are being overrun' (it was decades later before I knew the message did get through). Then did my best to wreck my No. 18 Radio Set.

'We could hear the enemy shouting to us to come out quickly, I think I was about the third to emerge. Outside there was the body of one of my pals, Philpot, who had been shot through the head and killed.

'As we came out, about twelve or fourteen of us including the CO Lieutenant Colonel Sym, our Intelligence Officer, who was a young Lieutenant and a Forward Observation Officer from the artillery, he was a major, who said it was the second time he had been taken prisoner, as he been taken prisoner in the first world war.

The house on the right is where Ernest was taken POW on
29 March 1945, near Dinxperlo

'I could see a German Parachute Regiment around us. I was singled out
and a young paratrooper brandishing a Luger 9mm pistol came to deal with
me. He was probably only sixteen and ordered me to throw my helmet and
the rest of my equipment down, he then searched me, flinging my reading
glasses to the ground and stamped his jackboot on them.

'What happened next could have been disastrous; I had earlier, rather
foolishly, picked up a pair of German wire cutters which were excellent,
they were in a leather holster stuck in my trouser belt and I had completely
forgotten about them in the melee. My captor suddenly spotted them and
said 'Ah Kamerad' as he jabbed his Luger into my stomach. For a moment
time stood still - the message was clear - but I cannot remember what I
thought. Luckily, he didn't press the trigger.

'We were then marched at rifle point down the road. Later my friend
Ray Nicolls said he was watching me from near the bridge. As we were
marched down the road, alongside the river, we were amazed to see
numerous German Paras up to their waists in the water sheltering from the
Seaforths fire. We were completely unaware that the rest of the battalion
was very much intact and had the German Paras pinned down.

'A number of us were herded into the ground floor of a single-storey house
overlooking the small river and shortly afterwards the Huns came and set
up a Spandau belt-fed machine gun on the table, presumably to engage
our lads on the nearby bridge. But they never opened fire.

'I was sitting on the floor by the open door to the garden when one of our captors pointed his rifle at me and the fellow next to me, he then pointed to a German lying wounded about fifteen yards out in the garden. It left both of us in no doubt what was expected of us; to bring the [German] casualty in from a spot that was under the Seaforths fire. It was obvious that we had no alternative so hoping for the best we dragged him undercover and his pals [the Germans] laid him on a table and cut his uniform open.

'He had been shot through his stomach and died about ten minutes later, he was one of their senior NCOs a sergeant major I think, so an experienced soldier.

'We were then herded into the cellar. After a while, we were offered a bacon sandwich, but it was rancid, and we all said thank you very much, but did not take one.

'Then it all went very quiet, and we wondered what was happening above. Suddenly we heard a voice shouting 'Is there any British down there? Our blokes had come looking for us. We all yelled out 'Yes'. I could never remember the time scale, but it was probably about two hours, so much seemed to be happening, or was I too scared perhaps - Probably.

'Once out of the cellar I was told to go and find my kit, which was exactly where it was stripped from me earlier that day.

'Later it became obvious that only the Battalion HQ had been in our little aside and the rest of the Battalion was intact and had dealt with the situation. We lost a number of men that day, Philpot being one of them. Little was said about it afterwards and we just got on with the next task.

The battalion lost fourteen men that day; as Ernest was good friends with John Philpot, the signals sergeant allowed him to go to his burial, which was close to the bridge where he was killed and Ernest along with the Battalion HQ were overrun. John William Philpot was 26 years old when killed on 29th March 1945, the son of William James Philpot and Margaret Alice Philpot, of Olney, Buckinghamshire. John Philpot was later re-buried in the Reichswald Forest War Cemetery, which was established after the war when burials were gathered from across western Germany. Today it is the largest Commonwealth War Graves Commission cemetery in Germany.

'A day or so later we moved a little to secure the bridgehead. I was sitting on a doorstep very close to a dirt road when I was disturbed by the roar of a motorbike engine; to my utter shock a motorbike and side-car passed a few feet away containing a driver and passenger in German uniform - C'est la Guerre - Surprised all.

'The Dutch border was close by and a few days later our unit moved some distance north to Enschede in northern Holland. Two of us were billeted with a delightful couple who put us up in a very comfortable bedroom. He was an engine driver, which was not very healthy as he had been strafed by allied aircraft, but they were very kind and gentle people. What a joy after sleeping rough for weeks, I often regret not noting their names and details to thank them for their hospitality.

'One afternoon the town was bedecked with flags, and we saw the arrival of Prince Bernhardt, the husband of Queen Wilhelmina, to join the locals in their celebrations of liberty. A unique occasion and long remembered, the population were ecstatic, remembering they had been starving and we dropped food to them.

'The rumour filtered through that the war was nearly over and we had finished. Two days later that situation was dashed, and we were ordered to be prepared to move at any time. The retreating Germans were blowing every bridge and culvert to delay our advance and it was our role to prevent this and get behind them. So, we moved back to Germany.

'We forced marched about 19 km from Vechta to Goldenstedt through the night, trying to get behind the German lines - I think they were the towns although I was so tired it did not register easily. As we marched, we came across a German car with four soldiers in, a few shots and they came out. At dawn, we approached a village to find several 20mm cannons mounted on wooden poles but not manned.

'I later learned that they were from [aircraft] fighters and that they should have been manned by a Luftwaffe unit, who we discovered were still in bed. What fun our lads had in digging them all out still in their underpants, or less, with not a shot being fired.

'We moved on and consolidated our position, it was good agriculture farming country, and I dug in at the front garden of a lovely farmhouse and rested all morning. In the middle of the afternoon, I was disturbed by *a movement from some shrubs, then out from under the shrubs emerged a German officer, a Colonel, with his hands up to surrendered.*

'He must have been there for several hours only a few feet away hoping to get away somehow. He was quickly whisked away, within a quarter of an hour - What a day.

'Then into the outskirts Bremerhaven but this was largely taken by the Canadians, I think.

Ernest, taken 5th May 1945 at Bremervorde the day after the cessation of hostilities

'We were then moved to take the small town of Bremervorde to the East, apart from some shellfire I remember having to race to a narrow river and crossing a special bridge thrown over by one of the specialist tanks, one of the funnies.

'We approached the bridge by a shallow ditch and one of my lasting memories was having to stride over the dead body of one of our men.

'He was surely the last man of the whole division to lay down his life, because the fighting was over the very next day, we got ordered to do nothing unless attacked, it may have been 4th May 1945.

'We then moved up to Cuxhaven at the mouth of the Elbe to take the surrender, as we approached the town, in battle order, the German Marines marched out four abreast all spick and span to surrender - a very moving occasion long to be remembered.

'The marines were immaculate with polished jackboots and uniforms, probably to impress us, they saluted every officer, I doubt if we were in the mood to be impressed. We were in battle order and far from smart.

'The next day we moved a few miles up the river to be billeted in a village called Altenbruch, where we stayed for at least four months.

'During that time my colleague, Ray, and I received intensive training and tests to qualify as Infantry Signallers, the job we had already done in action; however, it meant increased pay.

'We did not get any back-dated pay. But we were given our Infantry Signallers Badge after the course, the crossed flags.

'Then one morning I was placed on COs orders for no apparent reason, it usually meant trouble. What had I done wrong? However, it was to offer me the chance to go back over to England to Kent to be commissioned and I had twenty-four hours to decide. But I had to sign on for at least another four years, the colonel even said he would like me back in his battalion.

'After due thought, I appeared again before Colonel Sym to say no. He then spent several minutes telling me what an opportunity I was missing.

'I was granted fourteen days leave in September, when I returned, the Battalion had moved to guard a camp holding SS members and German personnel suspected of war crimes at Sandbostel. This had previously been a camp for British POWs and a concentration camp. Near our billet was a huge grave said to hold 3,000 bodies.

'In October, my battalion the 5th Seaforths were disbanded. I was posted as a signaller from a battalion raised at Wick in Caithness to the 2nd Battalion Devonshire Regiment, 7th Armoured Division - The Desert Rats. Stationed in Spandau West Berlin, close to where Hess was in prison.

'West Berlin was little damaged, they employed us with schemes and sporting activities. Shows and theatre companies were visiting from home, and I enjoyed three visits to the Berlin Opera House to see the Sadlers Wells Opera Company perform and several musical groups which were enjoyable.

'In the New Year, I got a short leave to a camp in Denmark. It was in the southeast at a place called Kolding and we had very good warm rooms, snow was on the ground, and it was very cold. One day we had an interesting trip to a small island in the Baltic on a German small in-shore minesweeper which ploughed through the ice about one inch thick.

'But one intriguing incident I remember occurred when travelling one of the three Autobahns which gave access to Berlin. I was in an open transport truck, and it was very cold in December. The truck developed engine trouble and the Sergeant in charge decided to leave the Autobahn to seek shelter for the night as it was getting dark.

'We soon found a local farmhouse, but the residents were very reluctant to admit us. Understandable as this was well in the Russian Zone and who knows what the results would have been for them and us, had we been found there. They made us amazingly comfortable, and I spent my first night ever in a duvet.

'They were desperately short of soap, so we left all our supplies with them. The next morning early the truck driver solved the problems and we proceeded to Berlin to be received by the Military Police in one hell of a row. The Sergeant should not under any circumstances have left the Autobahn but waited to be picked up. I often wonder what happened to him.

'Latter, I was offered a sergeant rank to take over the library, or I could take my demob. Ray took the sergeant's job at a German Cavalry Barracks in Berlin near Spandau. I decided to go home.

'In early February, following COs Orders I was released and transferred to the depot of the Devonshire Regiment at Plymouth.

'I left by train via the Hook of Holland and Harwich, arriving the next day. Twenty-four hours later I had collected my demob suit and headed home.

Ernest said goodbye to Ray as he left Berlin, he has not seen or heard from him since, and he also bid a farewell to Germany and the Army.

'I was demobbed on 8th February 1946 and given a month's leave, my parents were living in Swadlincote, I presented myself to the education officer in Burton-on-Trent, he offered me a job teaching, I started on 1st March at Branston Road School, they took children to the age of fourteen and I got the job of a science teacher. After one term I was offered another teaching post. I never changed my career for the rest of my working life.

'Then I moved to a school in Nottingham and stayed for a year, petrol rationing was a bit of a problem with thirty miles a day on my motorbike,

I had spent my money on a Triumph Twin. After this, I got a job in Swadlincote and stayed there for ten years, until 1960.

'I got married on 12th May 1951, at Hartshorne, near Swadlincote, my best man was my brother-in-law, Ken Moorcroft, who was a teacher in Hucknall. My wife was an infant schoolteacher and a reception teacher. I met her at what was then known as the matrimonial agency in Swadlincote, which is the young conservatives club. Her name was Audrey, Doreen Audrey Dolman. Her father had been a regular sailor, in the Royal Navy, from 1910 until 1924 then the Geddes Axe cut the forces and he was forced out.

'Audrey was born in 1926, the same age as The Queen. During the war, she was in college training in Whitelands College in Putney, which was bombed, and she was evacuated, with her elder sister, to Bede College in Durham, then after the war, she returned, for her second year to Putney.

'Sadly, we lost a daughter who died at a month old which was a big tragedy for us. We then had a son, Peter, born thirteen months later. Then three years later we had another son who died at six weeks old. Our marriage was so secure and sound we came through that, she said to me after we lost our second child that we must be in this together and we were.

'Peter is sixty-seven now, he has retired from being a design engineer working with about seventy men, on high precision stainless steel pressings for the likes of Rolls Royce and British Nuclear Fuels.

'He has been divorced and he married again, a widow with two children, I can remember teaching her first husband who sadly died at just twenty-eight. Now they have two of their own children and I have three great-grandchildren.

'I retired after teaching after twenty-six years at Wilsthorpe School in Long Eaton, it was 1985, I was aged sixty. I was head of craft design and technology. Audrey retired in 1983, she was the deputy head of an infant school in Long Eaton.

'In my younger days I did quite a bit of rock climbing, soon after coming out of the army, but when I got married my wife did not like the idea, so together we did a lot of fell walking. We have done all the peaks in the Lake District, except Great Gable.

'Then we would walk in Derbyshire every Monday, summer or winter, my favourite being Kinder Scout, which can be a bit barren. Or the top end of Dovedale when we would park at Hartington.

'Together we camped, then we caravanned and then we stayed in hotels.

Audrey sadly passed away last year, they had been married for seventy years and two days, to which Ernest commented.

'No other woman would have put up with me for seventy days, let alone over seventy years.

Ernest now lives alone but is thankful for the support he gets from his son and daughter-in-law, he cooks, some of which he says is not fit for human consumption.

Before I left, I asked him one final question; Ernest, you are now almost ninety-seven years old, you have had a long busy, very active and full life, is there anything you would put that down to?

'First and foremost, my wife, we could fall out twenty times a day, but it would only last for a few seconds, it was her guidance that helped, which I asked for all the time, which I now miss.

'I was lucky to be busy, I enjoyed walking, and playing golf and I still have a workshop where I still do cabinet making.

'But above all, you need something to do - All the time.

Matt Limb

'At last a battlefield tour guide that takes you to the battlefield ... not the memorials and museums of the battle'

It is hard to remember when my passion for British military history started.

Some of my early memories are reading books about the epic events of World War One & World War Two, plus speaking to veterans from both wars.

But whatever that date it has set my life on a course that continually takes me back to the battlefields, on which our forefathers grappled with the enemy in hand-to-hand combat.

Sir Winston Churchill once said that *'battles are the punctuation marks in this country's history'* I have been following that history for many years.

From the beaches of D Day to the trenches of World War One, along with some of the lesser known, but equally important, campaigns that form our history and its *'punctuation marks'.*

Today the visitors I take to explore the battlefield vary from relatives with a personal interest in a great uncle or grandfather, who simply want to know what it was their forefathers endured; to groups of people who want to understand and pay respect to a lost generation.

Whatever your reason, a visit to the battlefield will help you understand the battle and the men who fought there, in the *'punctuation'* marks of our history.

Matt Limb OBE TD   www.mlbft.co.uk

Author's Acknowledgments

A book of this nature and character needs the support and help of many people, without whom it would not have been possible to start researching or writing. Many individuals sent me notes and messages about a possible World War Two veteran, often outlining their stories, to each one of you, my sincere thanks.

Thanks also to the Royal British Legion, who have for over one hundred years helped, supported, campaigned - but above all remembered veterans. To the many branches and individuals who have helped in my search for veterans, who were able, willing and happy to tell their stories, I cannot thank you enough.

A special thanks must go to Paul Scott of the Ilkeston Branch, whom I met by chance, as we discussed the notion of this book. Without Paul's encouragement and support, this book would have never been finished.

But above all, the biggest thank you goes to the veterans of World War Two for sharing their time and telling their stories. At times, this was full of humour and joy, at others, it was pricked with sadness, my thanks to you for allowing your story to be remembered and shared.

BS - #0004 - 081122 - C10 - 234/156/10 - PB - 9780995781627 - Matt Lamination